Jesus Christ is Lord

by

Harold Paul Sloan

First Fruits Press
Wilmore, Kentucky
c2015

Jesus Christ is Lord : being a series of lectures given in part at the winter convocation of Asbury Seminary and Asbury College, in conjunction with the dedication of the Estes Memorial Chapel, January, 1954 by Harold Paul Sloan.

First Fruits Press, ©2015
Previously published: Louisville, Ky.: Pentecostal Publishing Company, ©1955

ISBN: 9781621712268 (print), 9781621712152 (digital), 9781621712275 (kindle)

Digital version at http://place.asburyseminary.edu/firstfruitsheritagematerial/101/

First Fruits Press is a digital imprint of the Asbury Theological Seminary, B.L. Fisher Library. Asbury Theological Seminary is the legal owner of the material previously published by the Pentecostal Publishing Co. and reserves the right to release new editions of this material as well as new material produced by Asbury Theological Seminary. Its publications are available for noncommercial and educational uses, such as research, teaching and private study. First Fruits Press has licensed the digital version of this work under the Creative Commons Attribution Noncommercial 3.0 United States License. To view a copy of this license, visit http://creativecommons.org/licenses/by-nc/3.0/us/.

For all other uses, contact:

First Fruits Press
B.L. Fisher Library
Asbury Theological Seminary
204 N. Lexington Ave.
Wilmore, KY 40390
http://place.asburyseminary.edu/firstfruits

Sloan, Harold Paul, 1881-1961.
    Jesus Christ is Lord : being a series of lectures given in part at the winter convocation of Asbury Seminary and Asbury College, in conjunction with the dedication of the Estes Memorial Chapel, January, 1954 / by Harold Paul Sloan.
    189 pages ; 21 cm.
    Wilmore, Ky. : First Fruits Press, ©2015.
    Reprint. Previously published: Louisville, KY : Pentecostal Publishing Company, ©1955.
    ISBN: 9781621712268 (pbk)
    1. Jesus Christ – Person and offices. 2. Jesus Christ – Lordship. I. Title.
BT201 .S622 2015   232

Cover design by Wesley Wilcox

asburyseminary.edu
800.2ASBURY
204 North Lexington Avenue
Wilmore, Kentucky 40390

First Fruits Press
The Academic Open Press of Asbury Theological Seminary
204 N. Lexington Ave., Wilmore, KY 40390
859-858-2236
first.fruits@asburyseminary.edu
asbury.to/firstfruits

JESUS CHRIST IS LORD

by Harold Paul Sloan

Being a series of lectures, given in part at the winter convocation of Asbury Seminary and Asbury College, in conjunction with the dedication of the Estes Memorial Chapel, January, 1954.

Pentecostal Publishing Company
Box 774, Louisville, Ky.

Copyright, 1955
PENTECOSTAL PUBLISHING COMPANY
Louisville, Kentucky

FOREWORD

By President John Alexander Mackay
of Princeton

This book, written by a beloved minister of the Methodist Church, who for years wielded a potent editorial pen in the direction of a great religious journal, is a moving contribution to the ever contemporary theme of the Lordship of Jesus Christ.

The four words which form the title of Dr. Sloan's book,s *Jesus Christ Is Lord,* are the most momentous four words ever spoken. The affirmation which they make constitutes the first, and at the same time, the most basic Christian creed. This creed is not a formula which grew out of academic discussion; it arose out of a conflict of thought, and still more, out of a tremendous experience which came to the lives of Christians in the apostolic era.

This thrilling affirmation is sounded in Paul's great Letter to the Philippians. Paul wrote the Philippian letter in a dungeon in the imperial city of the Caesars. The man from Tarsus proclaimed that one day every tongue would "confess that Jesus Christ is Lord to the glory of God the Father." (Phil. 2:11) Why? Because God was for the earlier Christians a greater "lord" than the Roman Emperor and was one with the "Lord God of Israel." A great New Testament scholar has made the remark that to grasp the meaning of these words and to apply their implications to thought and life would bring back in our time the atmosphere of the apostolic era.

The words of this earliest confession of faith confront us with the fact that the Christian religion is the religion of a Person. The other great religions of mankind are essentially religions of ideas. They have their personalities, of course, their sages and their prophets, their mystics and their saints. But those religious leaders do not belong to the very substance of the truth which they proclaimed. Not so with Christianity. It is no exaggeration to say that Christianity is Christ. While the Christian religion, more perhaps than any other great world faith, has given birth to ideas and to great systems of ideas, mere ideas do not constitute the essence of the Christian faith. Whether the structure of Christian truth is set forth as a building, it is Christ who is the foundation; whether it be presented in the biological figure of a body, Jesus Christ is the Head of the Body. There come to mind in this connection the memorable words of the greatest Christian saint that Christianity in India has produced, the famous Sadhu Sundar Singh. Asked on one occasion by a group of friends belonging to other religions what it was that he had found in Christianity which he could not have found in the historic religions of his country, Sundar Singh answered, "I have found Christ."

Nothing is more needed in our time than to recover the sense of the centrality of Christ for the thought and life of our generation. It is no exaggeration to say that the Bible is a book about Christ. He is the core of the Bible, the messages of the Book. He is also the clue to the Bible's meaning. It is only in the measure in which the Bible is read in the light of Christ, and interpreted in terms of the experience which comes when life is surrendered to Christ, that the Bible can be truly understood. In these last decades of Christian history, many a controversy could have been avoided, or at least would have been differently oriented and carried on, if this truth had been remembered.

It is impossible to overemphasize the central place which Jesus Christ has in the religion which bears his name, and the equally central place which he should have in Christian thought, in Christian life, and in the Christian Church. The true starting point of the Christian religion, let it be said, is not God or man but the God-man, Jesus Christ. This is a profound truth which must never be forgotten.

Today, however, we confront a strange situation when we affirm that "Jesus Christ is Lord." In some circles, alas, the term "Lord" has a soft, sentimental, sanctimonious sound; in other circles, it has a sinister association. These last years of totalitarian rule in both Fascist and Communist countries have publicized "lords" who exercise tyrannic rule. For that reason, it is important to re-think and to rehabilitate this great designation of Jesus Christ. It is necessary to challenge the members of our churches, and the citizens of our time, with the meaning of the Lordship of Jesus Christ, to confront them with the tremendous fact that He is Lord.

What is meant when we say "Jesus Christ is Lord"? He is the Lord of thought and the Lord of life, Lord of death and the Lord of history. Christ is the Lord of thought. Affirmations regarding the meaning of God and man, of life and destiny, can only be made in the light of Him who is Himself the truth. Christ is also the Lord of life. It is He who confers true life upon men and nations. Christ is the Lord of death, which He conquered and made the great "Mother," from whom came forth, and continues to come forth, new and transfigured life. Christ is also the Lord of history. He controls the whole historical process. It is He who unseals the scroll of the future, and who "shall reign forever and ever."

The several chapters of Dr. Sloan's book move forward from the affirmation of Christ's Deity, through the episode of His birth, onwards through studies on the meaning of His Cross, Resurrection, Ascension, His coming again, and His final triumph. The volume reveals a devout and scholarly author whose style is lucid and poetic. Because of the wealth of telling illustrations with which the text is studded, lay men and women will find the several chapters easy and attractive reading.

Deeply impressive is the author's reference to his own first experience of Christ at the turn of the present century. His reference to that experience puts him in the great tradition of evangelical literary work in which a man writes because he "cannot but speak the things which he has seen and heard." The sense of Christ as a living Presence has marked Dr. Sloan's own life and witness. It has given him the poise and the passion, the balance and the ardour, which have marked the personal witness of the saintly author of this volume.

The present writer is particularly happy that the distinguished author of this book feels that within history itself, and not simply at the end of history or beyond history, there will be a glorious consummation of the Gospel and work of Jesus Christ. There is clear evidence in the Biblical records that within the annals of time we shall witness a worthier expression of Christ and the Gospel than has yet been manifested in human history. For not only at history's end, but also within it's course, it shall become manifest that Jesus Christ the Lord is the hope of the world.

—JOHN A. MACKAY

Dedicated to the Lordship of Jesus Christ and in grateful recognition of that long line of witnesses whose spirit energized worship has maintained Him always living and contemporary.

"*Among these, this dedication particularly recognizes Ralph A. Earl and his wife Elizabeth, whose generous devotion to Christian truth has been and is most creative.*"

CONTENTS

CHAPTER		PAGE
1	Jesus Christ	13
II	The Wonder of Christmas	33
III	The Transfiguration	46
IV	The Triumphal Entry	58
V	The Cross — God So Loved	67
VI	The Resurrection	86
VII	The Meaning of the Ascension	96
VIII	The Gift of the Holy Spirit to Abide	105
IX	The Out — Resurrection —That Out From Among the Dead	124
X	The Consummation Within History	138
XI	The Second Coming of Christ	158
XII	The Consummation Beyond History	172

JESUS CHRIST

HEBREWS 1:1-2

"God, who at sundry times, and in diverse manners, spake in times past unto the fathers by the prophets, hath in these last days spoken to us by His Son, whom He made heir of all things, by whom also He made the worlds."

It is impossible not to be thrilled by the grandeur of the New Testament. It constantly deals with such immense ideas as God, Righteousness, Death, Judgment, the Resurrection, and Eternal Life. Man's aspiring soul, consequently, is immediately at home the moment he begins to read it.

The text introduces us to another one of these immense ideas—Revelation. God has long been speaking to men. The forms of His disclosures have been various. He spoke to the fathers through the prophets, using almost every conceivable form of literature and experience; but, now climactically, He has spoken to men in His Son—that Son whom He hath appointed heir of the universe, and by whom also He constituted it.

This sublime Son is known to men in history as Jesus of Nazareth. In the Greek text of Hebrews, He is called just "a son"; but in view of the description of Him which follows immediately, it is evident that the designation "His Son" is a better expression of the author's meaning. The Jesus of Nazareth of our text is evidently more than "a son" because no mere creature would be capable of occupying the station assigned to Him as heir of all things and the creator of the universe.

The Epistle to the Hebrews was probably written shortly before the destruction of Jerusalem in the year 70. Consequently Jesus was definitely bracketed with God at that early date. But the same is true also of the Epistles of St. Paul; and the first of these to be written carries us back almost to the year 50. There are, however, two records in the book of *Acts* which show this high conception of Christ's person to have been in expression at the very beginning of the Christian Church. Stephen prayed to Jesus at the very instant of his passing (7:60), and Peter classified Him as one closely related to God who had been sent into time for redemptive purposes, in his first Christian sermon preached on the Day of Pentecost of the year 30 (2:37f).

The probability is that the disciples had some foregleaming of this understanding of Christ's person even before the Cross, and that from the time of the Resurrection, it had been an admitted truth among them. You can feel their thrilling wonder as they lay hold upon this immense understanding in the opening exclamations of *St. John's Catholic Epistle*. He wrote: "That which was from the beginning, which we have heard, which we have seen with our eyes, which we have looked upon and our hands have handled—I am referring to the Logos who shares God's Eternal Life; and the Eternal Life was truly manifested, and we have seen, and witness, and proclaim to you the Life,

JESUS CHRIST IS LORD

the Eternal Life, which was with the Father, and was made manifest to us" (1:1,2).

St. John's sense of the majesty and reality of this great experience almost defied expression. His conviction was so great, and his emotions so flooding that they exploded his sentences. He had to interrupt himself with exclamations of wonder and certainty—Yes, the Eternal Life, which had been from everlasting, had been made manifest within time; and common men, of whom he was one had heard and seen and handled Him.

This is the immense truth which crowned Israel's unique national history; and it is indeed sublime beyond exaggeration. It is staggering. There is nothing else in experience with which it can be compared save the infinite aspirations of the human soul. The fact of Christ and the reach of human aspirations are both infinite. Christ corresponds to and fulfills man's soul; but He towers above every other value known to experience. He is like the giant sequoia trees, which tower above the brush which grows at their roots.

Jesus Christ and the aspiring souls of men! And if the aspiring souls of men are ever to be fulfilled, such a figure as Jesus Christ had to appear some time within history. The record of the Gospels is that He did appear in the year 747 A.U. (Anno Urbus), or at the end of the year 7 B.C., according to our familiar Christian chronology.

I want to present Jesus' amazing figure under four descriptive words; which do at least partially summarize His glory—Jesus is an *indisputable fact,* an *incomparable fact,* an *inexhaustible fact;* and then at last, through faith, He becomes a *fact inbreathed.*

Jesus is an indisputable fact. He did not appear long ago when history was scanty and myth abounded, but just yesterday in the midst of the abounding Greco-Roman civilization. He was the contemporary of Caesar Augustus, Seneca, Gamaliel, Saul of Tarsus—ranking personalities of the first century. Professor John Scott calls Him the best certified personality of His times.* His life, death, and the witness to His resurrection produced the universal Christian Church. They produced also the Gospels—the most translated, and best read literature of the world and of the ages. His influence has changed history, making possible a tremendous advance in human dignity and freedom—evidently one of the fundamental motifs of the universe.

Assuming that there is such a thing as Truth, and therefore such a thing as meaning, the universe is manifestly a great inclusive unity advancing toward freedom. The life, death, and resurrection of Jesus of Nazareth served the progress of this human dignity and freedom with creative power. Before these events chattel slavery was almost universal, effective free government literally unknown, irreverence for human personality a common attitude, despair all embracing. The fact is the fear of death haunted the people of the ancient world. They buried their dead with institu-

---

*Professor John Scott, formerly head of the department of Greek at Northwestern University in his volume, "We Would Know Jesus."

tionalized wailing, and habitually engraved "Farewell Forever" upon their tombs. The impact of Jesus, however, changed all this. The primitive Church made the manumission of slaves an important ritual occasion. It affirmed universal human dignity, and refused all recognition to the degrading gladiatorial shows. It illumined death with infinite hope; and after its Gospel became the intimate possession of believers generally, at the Reformation, effective free government burst out of its life as grass and flowers do out of the moist warm earth in spring.

To call in question the historic reality of Jesus of Nazareth is thus completely absurd. No one who lives in the age of the atom bomb would be absurd enough to doubt the historic reality of Albert Einstein, and it is equally absurd to live in the midst of the dignity and freedom Jesus made possible, and yet deny His reality. Without Him and the apostolic witness to His victory over death, our modern world never could have burst out from within the despair and slavery of paganism.

Jesus, then, is completely indisputable. His universal Church, His universal Gospel, and His creative influence upon civilization exclude any possibility of an intelligent question as to His reality. He stands in history like some majestic rock of Gibraltar completely dominating the scene. But there is an additional witness to Him, even yet hardly appreciated, which makes Him literally unescapable. It is that a group of secular writers of the first and early second centuries had described Him, and that their portrait markedly agrees with that preserved in the Gospels. They describe Him as a teacher of high religious and moral truth, who gathered about Him disciples, wrought miracles (called sorceries), empowered His disciples to perform the same, and was crucified on the eve of a Passover which was also the Sabbath Day. They note His open empty sepulchre, and call attention to the confidence of His followers that they can attain to immortality through relation to Him. They describe Him as the founder of a new religion. These secular documents are The Mara, a history by Tacitus, a history by Josephus, an official letter by the governor of Bithynia to Trajan, the Hebrew Mishna, and some of the writings of Lucian. If it should be objected, that these writings have been called in question, the answer is instant: This is the case only with respect to the reference to Jesus in Josephus; and that reference, as it has been made use of here, is admitted to be authentic by Professor Klausner of Jerusalem University.

Jesus, then is indisputable, but He is also incomparable. Men do sometimes bracket Him with other religious leaders. I have seen Him thus bracketed with Moses, Buddha, Socrates. These comparisons, however, are intellectually quite irresponsible. No one who deeply knows the life of Jesus and at the same time the lives of these men could think of making such comparisons. The glory of Jesus' life bursts out of such a bracketing as new wine does out of old bottles.

Take Moses; he was unquestionably a massive character. Nevertheless, he cannot be bracketed with Jesus, for Moses once committed murder, and was afterward so embarrassed by the circumstances that he fled from Egypt becoming a fugitive from the law in the desert of Midian. Nor can we excuse Moses as immature when he committed this crime. He was not immature. He was already older than Jesus was when He was crucified. Moses saw a wrong being committed, which he was right in resenting, but which he was wrong in opposing by an even greater wrong. Moses allowed his indignation to make him forget his obligation to respect even those who are evidently wrong; and this failure necessarily places him in a different classification from Jeus. Had there been such a failure in the life of Jesus, His impact upon the centuries would have been totally different. Jesus never failed in poise; He never forgot that He owed it to reverence every personality, even those which were deeply sinful. So He reverenced the woman taken in adultery, the robber dying on the cross beside Him, and the sadistic crowd which mocked His dying agony. There is no record that Jesus' moral poise ever failed, and this immense difference between Him and Moses makes it intellectually irresponsible to bracket them together.

As to comparing Buddha with Jesus, we know so little about the former that there is quite no basis for any comparison. The *Lalita Vistara,* which provides our earliest account of Buddha was not written until a century after his death, and may not have been written until eight centuries after his death. Manifestly, such a writing cannot be looked upon as historically significant. The fact is no one who has read it will make the suggestion that it is historically significant. Its stories are constantly both morally purposeless and fantastic. No one who has intelligently read both the *Lalita* and the *Gospels* will think of comparing them. Buddha, thus, is little more than a name and a teaching; and to bracket him with Jesus is once again intellectually irresponsible.

Coming to Socrates, the comparison is again unimpressive. Socrates was a good man and a noble teacher, but that is all. Repeatedly he came short by the highest standards of human goodness. Thus, he was extremely inconsiderate of his wife, when she came to the Athenian jail to bid him goodby just before he drank the hemlock. She had come with their infant son for a farewell greeting, and Socrates, instead of going to her, sent one of the young men, saying, "Send her home." He did not want her tears to interrupt the elevation of their philosophical conversation. Or again, there are sections in his defense before the Athenian court that would almost have to be called "smart", they are so lacking in that humility and reserve one is compelled to admire in Jesus. Socrates, indeed, lived a courageous life, and died an elevated death; but it would be completely impossible to worship him. Had Jesus in life and death and resurrection attained no higher than Socrates did, there could never have been either a universal Christian Church or a universal Gospel.

Jesus, then, is literally incomparable. In his later years Napoleon became conscious of Jesus' uniqueness, and discoursed upon it with his suite during his exile on St. Helena. The Emperor recognized that no other character in history could be stood beside Jesus. He was basically different.

But what was the spring of this remarkable uniqueness? Certainly it was not either His virgin birth or His miracles, in both of which I rejoice firmly to believe. Jesus' uniqueness was very much more basic. It was the reality of His God-saturated consciousness. Jesus was almost continuously in the Presence. That is, whenever He was conscious of Himself, He was conscious also of the intimate nearness of His Father. His Father was as near Him as Himself. His Father indwelt Him, enriched Him, illumined Him, and guided Him. Jesus was thus Himself, plus. He was never alone. He was always both completed and enlarged by the fellowship of His Father.

St. John properly understood this unique elevation of Jesus, and described it for us in his account of the Saviour's washing of His disciples' feet. He wrote, "Jesus, knowing that the Father had given all things into his hands, and that he came from God and went to God", rises from supper, girds Himself with a towel, and performs the slave's office for the Twelve, washing their street soiled feet (St. John 13:3f). Notice that St. John did not mean to say Jesus did these things in spite of His exalted Divine relationships. St. John saw Jesus doing these things precisely because of His Divine relationships. Jesus' infinite relationships lifted Him completely above the point of view which makes possible the sense of pride, humiliation, and sacrifice. All three of these attitudes are self-centered; and Jesus lived too inclusively to experience them. Jesus lived steadily in a world that was glorified by the evident presence of His Father, and His own life was constantly illumined and guided by His intimate disclosures. Consequently, He washed men's feet as readily as He died for them, and He did both with a feeling of life-fulfilling rapture.

This was the characteristic which made Jesus essentially different from all other men. He Himself put it into words in the closing exclamation of His great communion—"O righteous Father, the world hath not known thee; but I have known thee!" (John 17:25).

Several modern writers attempt to explain this tremendous God-consciousness of Jesus without the supernaturals of the Gospels. They stumble at the Virgin Birth, and say Jesus must have had an earthly father. They stumble at the Incarnation, and say Jesus must have begun as a mere human being just like any other human being. Finally, they stumble at the record of Jesus' sinlessness, and say He must have risen out of error and misconception into truth.

These writers think they have conceived a consistent figure, who starting at the strictly human level, achieved such a responsiveness to the Spirit that He became both God-conscious, and an effective expression of God. He came, in fact, so exceedingly close to God that His death on the Cross could be conceived as a Divine sacrifice.

There are several things which ought to be said about this modern explanation of Jesus. In the first place it is not new, for it was proposed and rejected as long ago as the third century. Men rejected it then, as they will reject it now, because the figure of Jesus

JESUS CHRIST IS LORD 23

so conceived is too small. He is too small to carry the weight of Jesus' immense self-consciousness. He is too small also to carry the weight of Jesus' redemptive responsibility.

There have been many men during the Christian centuries who have attempted to do what these writers tell us Jesus did. They have attempted to be completely obedient to the guidance of the Holy Spirit. But no one of them ever attained to anything even approximating the unique self-consciousness of Jesus. Survey swiftly just the names of a few of them. In the first century there were St. John and St. Paul. In the second century there were Ignatius and Polycarp. In the third Origen, Cyprian and Tertullian. In the fifth St. Ambrose and St. Augustine. In the eighth there was the glorious St. Boniface of Germany. In the twelfth there was St. Bernard of Clairvaux. In the sixteenth there was Martin Luther. In the eighteenth there was John Wesley. In the twentieth there have been and are such men as Professor Olin Alfred Curtis, Bishop James Bashford, Dr. Albert Schweitzer, and no one of these men ever made or was capable of making the amazing claims that were commonplace on the lips of Jesus. Jesus felt that He knew and expressed God so completely that to have seen Him was to have seen God. Such words upon the lips of St. Augustine, St. Bernard, Martin Luther, John Wesley would have seemed blasphemy. Wesley's final self estimate may fitly be taken as the self estimate of them all. He was standing at the very threshold of death. He said deliberately of himself, "Nothing I have done will bear looking at." His confidence was, "Jesus died for me."

As one reads these new-old speculations, one often wonders whether their authors ever attained to read and think existensially? Are they familiar either with the New Testament or with their own lives existensially? I speak for myself. This writer has undertaken to walk obediently in the light of the Holy Spirit for more than fifty years. He would not shrink from being measured by John Wesley's description of perfect love. Nevertheless, the confusion of his ideas and of his motives startle him. He often finds it necessary to suspend action, and leave some situation hung up until he can clarify his emotions, his motives, his soul. He used to think John Wesley extreme when he wrote, "Nothing I have done will bear looking at", but now he knows Wesley wrote with a morally sincere understanding of himself. No forgiven sinner can presume to stand self-approved in the presence of the glory of God. No forgiven sinner can ever exclaim with Jesus, Nobody knows me but God, and nobdy knows God but me (Matt. 11:27), or again, "O righteous Father, the world hath not known thee, but I have known thee" (St. John 17:25), or yet once more, "He that hath seen me hath seen the Father . . . Believe me that I am in the Father and the Father in me; or else believe me for the very works' sake" (St. John 14:9-11). Jesus' self-consciousness rises above ours so completely that our best does not even approach His. Yes, He is indeed incomparable.

Then, third, Jesus is inexhaustible. We have been thinking about Him, writing about Him, and worshipping Him these nineteen hundred years; and He is as gripping a reality today as He was nineteen hundred years ago. In 1909 President Charles Eliott, of Harvard, gave an address at the university in which he prophesied that the religion of the future would no longer stress creed and metaphysics. Instead he said, it would stress human understanding and service. President Eliott was of course repudiating those age old accents of historic Christianity which have continuously expressed its faith in the Deity of Jesus Christ, and in other transcendent values. President Eliott felt that this credal and metaphysical emphasis was largely meaningless, and that the religion of the future would leave these things behind.

Since President Eliott made this statement two generations have been born and two generations have in large part passed on. Many in those generations have shared also his convictions and promoted them, diminishing their emphasis upon creed and metaphysics. The first half of the twentieth century was indeed a period which magnified science and this-world values. Its leaders stressed altruism and service until these words became as familiar to our ears as the songs of birds in the mating season. Nevertheless, in spite of this emphasis upon the social, we have lived self-centeredly, and we have produced the extreme brutalities of Communism and Nazism. We have produced also a very considerable number of men with graduate degrees who have been willing to betray free institutions, and who have done so by conspiracy, treachery and lying.

A reaction, indeed, is now setting in; and during

the last twenty years there has been a very considerable turning back to Christ as the one hope of our age. The liberal weekly, *The Christian Century* gave large recognition to this intellectual reaction as long ago as the mid-thirties, and now in the middle fifties, Nathan M. Pusey, the present president of Harvard has openly repudiated the viewpoint of his predecessor, pointing out that a religion without creed and metaphysics is not adequate to meet the needs of men. Consequently, at the middle of the twentieth century, we are once again turning to history's inexhaustible Christ.

And how often the centuries have done this! Again and again, deceived by some illusion of human greatness, men have turned their back upon Christ. They have projected some proud self-sufficient advance; and then almost in a moment have arrived at disaster. The fruitage of their self-sufficient progress has been moral and social disintegration. Then bewildered and somewhat chastened, they have turned back to Christ again.

Thus the Italian Renaissance was the first fruitage of the great humanist advance. Men appreciated themselves as the masters of art and literature. They neglected the Gospel. They produced a harvest of immorality and social confusion. The reaction from this was the Reformation.

It was the same again with English Deism. It was born in the seventeenth century, and bore its disastrous social fruitage in the eighteenth. In the name of proud reason men repudiated all supernaturals, including Christ. The results were, morality was unfounded; the social decencies of life were forgotten;

manners became so corrupt that law could hardly be enforced. In a word, English democracy was almost destroyed. But happily, in the midst of this flippancy and confusion the Wesleyan Revival burst, and a great reaction to Christ began. Historians in considerable number tell us that this happy circumstance saved England from the ravages of the French Reign of Terror.

A third illustration of this same sequence of developments is now taking place. Western civilization had been unfounded by the projection into it of modern Rationalism, Naturalism, and Scientific Determinism. As a result Christian influence had declined, and Communism and Naziism had assumed command. The consequences have been shocking in the extreme. Civilization has been debased. Men and women have been killed like rats; and those leaders did not even call it murder; they were just liquidating a social liability.

Such was western civilization between the wars; but already before these bitter consequences had developed, the most recent reaction to Christ had begun. Karl Barth challenged the then contemporary point of view, and his challenge has developed into the neo-orthodox movement.

This pendular swing in history is arresting. Christ seems to be one pole of it; and the other is some form of human pride and self-sufficiency. At the Renaissance it was culture, in 18th century England it was philosophy, in the 20th century it has been modern man's pride in the magnificent accomplishments of science. The particular development seems to make no difference. Human pride evidently can take occasion in any new accomplishment, and then repudiate Christ—history's best—in the name of some very much smaller good. But inevitably when men have left Christ behind, they have built confusion and tragedy. Consequently, chastened, and for the moment wiser, they have turned back to Him again. There is only one condition to this sequence of reactions. The return to Christ always has to wait for some creative personality to spark it. There has to be a Luther, a Wesley, a Karl Barth, and if he does not appear the reaction to Christ may be greatly delayed.

Christ, then, is indeed inexhaustible. His impact lifted civilization to new and higher levels of possibility; but those levels can be neither possessed nor maintained without Him. When we turn our backs upon Him, civilization inevitably declines, notwithstanding we still know the elevation at which we were once able to live.

We come now to the fourth of our words, the one which affirms that the fact of Christ, when it is received with faith, becomes a *fact in-breathed*. This is the mystery of the New Birth—the Spirit's revelation of the infinite Presence within the believer's deepest consciousness (his self-consciousness).

We will come to this truth again, when we deal with the experience of the coming of the Holy Spirit to abide; but we want immediately to say a brief word about its significance and certainty.

There is a sharp difference between our relation to

JESUS CHRIST IS LORD

Jesus and our relation to other personalities in history. The writer has been a life long enthusiast with respect to George Washington, and that noble Christian patriot has greatly influenced his life; but never for one instant has George Washington come alive for him.

Jesus, on the contrary, did on a definite occasion come alive for him; and He has remained thus alive across five decades of living. There was a certain definite tremendous moment when Jesus became for him a living Presence, a Companion, a guiding Wisdom. The scientist's distinction between ordinary water and heavy water is no whit more definite than the distinction between an ordinary self-consciousness, and a Christ indwelt self-consciousness. Lecomte du Nouy discriminates between dinoflagellates which vegetated in their environment, and other dinoflagellates which responded to some upward impulse in nature and advanced to something higher. Some men vegetate in their temporal environment, and remain just dying men; but some men, responding to the fact of Christ in moral faith, become so profoundly identified with Him that both their deepest consciousness and the whole movement of their lives becomes markedly modified.

Review, now, some of the notable expressions this experience has produced. The hymns of the Church are a rich treasury of such expressions—"Jesus is real to me, yes, Jesus is real to me", "Still, still with Thee when purple morning breaketh", "Jesus kneel beside me in the dawn of day", "Abide with me, fast falls the eventide". Bernard of Clairvaux had such a powerful sense of the Saviour's presence that it produced a sweep of emotion which did not pause until he had written an enraptured song forty-eight stanzas long—"Jesus, Thou joy of loving hearts, Thou fount of life, Thou light of men"!

And so the fact of Christ does, through faith, by the Holy Spirit's revelation come alive. This is the climactic power of the Christian Gospel. Jesus, by the Spirit, becomes the constant companion of believing men; and His Presence enriches, satisfies, illumines, and guides them in every act of life. They never again act alone after the Presence is revealed in their deepest consciousness.

Confront, then, Jesus of Nazareth—a fact indisputable, a fact incomparable, a fact inexhaustible, a fact inbreathed! The solution of life is involved in this confrontation. At Wharton Memorial Church in Philadelphia it was long the regular practise to open worship with this introit:

> "The risen, living Christ, made forever contemporary by the believer's worship and the Holy Spirit's revelation, is the answer to every need of life, as Jesus said, 'And I, if I be lifted up, will draw all men unto me.'"

This is at once the power and philosophy of the Christian Gospel.

NOTE CONCERNING BASIC CREEDS AND THE NATURE OF THE INCARNATION

There are a number of modern thinkers who stumble at the Virgin Birth, the pre-existence of the

Son, and the reality of His sinlessness. These speculators regard themselves as having done a service to the Gospel by eliminating such details from its basic documents. They seem to think they have brought it into harmony with more certain intellectual values. This, however, is a serious mistake. What they have actually done is make a poor choice in basic creed, and then unfounded the Gospel by a piece of unrealistic, or as I would prefer to say, non-existential thinking.

The naturalistic creed to which they have given their devotion, *the affirmation of the absolute and all-embracing uniformity of nature,* is not only unproved and unprovable, but also it can be held only in open defiance to one of the basic insights of the human mind— *the insight that as moral men we are free, responsible personalities.* As free responsible personalities, we are necessarily transcendent to the alleged closed order of nature. The consequence is that human freedom violates philosophical naturalism as definitely as does virgin birth or any of the supernaturals of the Gospels.

The naturalistic creed, which these writers maintain, becomes thus not only unproved, and unprovable, but it becomes a creed held in the face of one of the deepest insights of the universal human mind. The creed of the Gospel, on the other hand, while as a creed it cannot be demonstrated, is nevertheless powerfully supported by a tremendously impressive historical witness. The apostolic Church maintained its witness and produced its Gospels with scrupulous care. It did not allow any intrusion even of a constructive imagination into their production. Books which contained such imagined details were rejected. These came to be known as the pseudographic gospels; and while some of them dated back almost to the apostolic age, they were rejected. Modern Criticism has not given sufficient weight to this great seriousness of the leaders of the Church in the apostolic age. When men are dying for their witness to a record, the moral earnestness with which they will maintain the purity of that record is something that can be assumed. Such men are not likely to be unrealistic or nonexistential thinkers. They are thinking in that atmosphere of high seriousness which the threat of martyrdom necessarily produces. These things being true, and they cannot be denied, we cannot set aside any important part of the Gospel record. The Virgin Birth, Sinlessness, and eternal Sonship of Jesus are such, and we modern men should be very slow to question them. Far from changing the New Testament to make it conform to our naturalistic creed, we should rather lift up the New Testament's witness to the reality of the transcendent as an added reason why the naturalistic creed is a poor moral choice.

THE WONDER OF CHRISTMAS

Psalms 42:1

"As the hart panteth after the waterbrook, so panteth my soul for Thee O God."

Isaiah 9:6

"For unto us a child is born, and unto us a Son is given; and the government shall be upon His shoulder; and His name shall be called Wonderful, Counsellor, The Mighty God, The Everlasting Father, and the Prince of Peace."

St. Matthew 1:18

"Now the birth of Jesus Christ was on this wise; when, as His mother Mary was espoused to Joseph, before they came together, she was found with Child of the Holy Ghost."

Life is either utterly wonderful or completely meaningless. There is no possible intermediate position between these extremes. If you accept our three texts as true, life is utterly wonderful. Our first text expresses the wonder of thirst that is intuitive in man's aspiring soul. Our second, expresses the wonder of God's promises of fulfillment given to man through the prophets. Our third, expresses the historic fact of fulfillment actually begun. These three tremendous realities constitute the wonder of Christmas.

And in what a perfect poem of lovely events God has enshrined Christmas! There were the angel visitations, the virgin motherhood, the flaming star, the humble shepherds, the kings from the East, and the white limestone grotto in the side of the Bethlehem hills.

We will begin our story with the star. Every year in Philadelphia at Advent the scientists of the Fels' Planetarium tell over again the story of the Christmas Star. St. Matthew records the fact of such a star. Wise Men had seen it in the East, and had ridden west, a thousand miles across the desert, to answer its summons.

Having arrived in Jerusalem, so the Gospels record, those men make inquiry for the highly destined Child, and learn that He will be born in Bethlehem. Immediately they renew their journey. They start south from the Holy City; and lo, just as they mount their camels, the mysterious star they had seen in the East, reappears before them, guiding them upon their way.

For centuries this Christmas Star remained a complete mystery. Men had no idea at all as to its nature. It was just a God given, supernatural star. It was so they thought of it, and asked nothing further. Then in the year 1603, the learned astronomer, Kepler, saw in the sky a brilliant conjunction of Jupiter, Saturn, and Mars. These planets came so close together that they shone almost as one star.

Kepler, himself, described this conjunction as a glowing spectacle. He was deeply impressed; and immediately, by one of those strange insights men do often experience, he asked himself, have I been looking at the Christmas Star? At once he began calculations to determine earlier occurrences of this same conjunction, and discovered that such had taken place in the years 7 and 6 B.C. in May, September, December

JESUS CHRIST IS LORD 35

and March. Kepler was disappointed. The dates were too early. However, they were near enough to be challenging, and so he made his calculations again.

We come now to our first sure fact with respect to the date of Nativity. It is that Archbishop Usher fixed that date almost five years too late. Jesus was born before Herod the Great died, and Herod's death took place on March the 13th, 750 A.U., that is four B.C.

The chronology in use in the Roman Empire when Jesus was born dated events from the time of the founding of the city of Rome. Thus Augustus Caesar, who was on the throne at the time of Nativity, began his reign in the year 727 A.U. Four years later, in the year 731 A.U., he instituted his first census of the Empire. From that time forward these enrollments recurred at each fourteenth year. Strikingly enough, in certain of the provinces, the method of making these enrollments conformed exactly to that described in St. Luke's Gospel. Citizens were ordered to return to their ancestral communities, and there enroll themselves. Census papers from the original enrollment in Egypt are now in possession of archaeologists, and furnish us with these details.

As must be known to every reader of the New Testament, the Gospels furnish us with no dates in the chronology of the Empire. Consequently Archbishop Usher had to calculate the date of Jesus' birth from the various chronological data which they do provide. His conclusion was that Jesus must have been born December 25th 754 A.U. and that Rome by consequence was established 754 B.C. But as we have already noted, Archbishop Usher's calculations of the time of Nativity set that date definitely too late, since Jesus was born during the life time of Herod the Great, and Herod died in 750 A.U. or four B.C.

This necessary correction in the date of Nativity brings us to within two years of the time fixed by Kepler for the earlier conjunction of Jupiter, Saturn and Mars. But there is quite no reason to suppose that Herod died within a matter of weeks after the birth of Jesus. The fact is the King, himself, thought that this notable birth might have taken place a number of months before he met the Wise Men. Consequently, in giving the order for the execution of Bethlehem's babes, he framed it: All male infants to at least two years of age (Matt. 2:16).

According to Herod's calculation the date of Nativity might have preceded his own death by more than two years, consequently Usher's calculation may need to be corrected by two years more. This would bring it back to December 25th 747 A.U. or 7 B.C. But if this calculation proves to be right, Kepler's star appeared exactly on time. May 747 A.U. should be approximately the time of the Annunciation. December 747 would be the actual time of the Birth. March 748 could be the time when the Wise Men saw the star when recommencing their quest of Messiah from Jerusalem.

The scientists at the Planetarium do not claim that these facts demonstrate the identity of the Christmas Star. They do, however, claim that they constitute a high degree of probability; and so annually they give this lecture upon Kepler's star to put the weight of scientific opinion behind the beautiful Christmas narratives of the Gospels.

And now against the background of this high probability, we will undertake to stand each lovely detail of the Nativity record.

After the Virgin had experienced her angelic vision and revelation, she very soon left Nazareth, and journeying south into the hill country of Judaea, sought for strength and encouragement in the fellowship of her cousin Elizabeth, who was also an expectant mother in connection with an angelic revelation. Mary continued with Elizabeth for several months, and only left her when the time was drawing near for her kinswoman's child to be born.

Mary's return to Nazareth, however, was not one to which she looked forward. Few, if any, of the people in Nazareth could be expected to believe her story. Indeed, Joseph, her betrothed, only believed it after receiving a heavenly revelation in a dream. Consequently, it must have been a great relief to the Virgin when Joseph announced to her that they would have to take the long journey to Bethlehem to be enrolled there for the census of the Empire.

It must have been about mid-December of the year 7 B.C., when Joseph and Mary set out. Their journey would be one roughly of a hundred miles. Mary, of course, would ride the family ass. Joseph would walk beside her carrying his heavy staff. It would take them about a week to make the journey; and so toward evening on the sixth day they would come in sight of

Bethlehem, and approach its kahn.

A village kahn in the year 7 B.C. was remote from what we today understand by an inn. It was in fact very much like our modern tourist camps. It was a walled enclosure, with a platform and roof along its four sides. Here the guests arranged their beds and carried on their ordinary camp activities. In the unroofed center they hitched their beasts and burned their small camp fires.

That night, however, even this limited hospitality failed the travelers from Nazareth. The kahn was crowded to capacity. There was absolutely no room. The keeper was sorry; but there was just so much room on the platforms, and every square cubit of it was already in use. There was, however, a grotto near by in one of Bethlehem's hills. It was often used as a stable; but it was dry and warm, and Joseph could make his wife quite comfortable in it.

Joseph took the keeper's suggestion, and easily found the grotto he indicated. It was not much work to sweep it out and make a straw bed for Mary upon the floor. The manger, cut in the rock of the floor, could easily be turned into a bed for the expected Child. Joseph did these things, made the Virgin comfortable in her blankets, and then went back to Bethlehem for help. This was soon found; and so leaving Mary and the midwife within, he established himself in the doorway of the grotto to guard against roaming animals and other night marauders.

St. Luke's account of the details of the census occasions no difficulty. We have already seen that Rome did not conduct censuses thus in some of the provinces of the Empire. The circumstance, however, that the Evangelist tells us that Cyrenius was governor of Syria when the census took place, does cause difficulty. It is a definite record that Sentius Saturnius was governor of Syria in 747-748 A.U. Indeed, Tertullian even states that the Nativity took place during his incumbency. How is it possible for Saturnius and Cyrenius both to be governors of Syria at the same time? Scholars have made two suggestions, either one of which will entirely solve the problem. First, they have suggested a joint administration of Saturnius and Cyrenius, similar to that of Mucianus and Vespasian. Second, they have suggested that Cyrenius, as military leader in Syria during his conquest of the Homonodenses, would automatically take precedence over the civil ruler. In view of St. Luke's recognized reputation for historical accuracy, some such solution of the seeming contradiction becomes highly probable.

That December night when Joseph and Mary came to Bethlehem the season was doubtless mild. Winter nights were often mild in Palestine, just as they are also in America. Weather conditions have a way of being different. Thus, during a recent winter, it was for several days warmer in Alaska than it was in Florida. There is consequently no reason why the Bethlehem shepherds may not have spent the night of December 24, 7 B.C. in the open as the Gospels say.

Consequently, we can picture them sitting about their camp fire, narrating such tales of adventure as they would know how to tell, when suddenly they are startled by the shining of a mysterious light. Instantly they are alerted, and exclaim one to another, What is this? But before any one can answer, they are even more startled by beholding a presence within the light. This presence speaks to them. He says, "Fear not: for behold I bring you good tidings of great joy, which shall be to all people. For unto you is born this day in the city of David a Saviour which is Christ the Lord."

Now the wonder of the vision rises still a degree higher. The solitary presence becomes a company, and a whole chorus of angels fill the night with mysterious music. They sing, "Glory to God in the highest, and on earth peace to the men of his good pleasure."

One should have no trouble quite simply to believe these beautiful records. Man's universal aspirations demand a transcendent world, and the indisputable facts of experience make it certain that beings from that world have from time to time made themselves manifest within our earth sphere. Joan of Arc unquestionably saw an angel during the winter of 1429. He appeared repeatedly, and he produced historic results that cannot be better explained than by affirming the reality of his appearances. Science has too long neglected to explore these transcendent data. Fortunately, now, a change has come, and these facts are being explored. Among the things that the atom bomb blew up is philosophical materialism, and it went a long way also toward discrediting philosophical naturalism. Consequently, if the transcendent is true there is no time when angels would more appropriately be made manifest than at Nativity and the Resurrection.

And so they appeared; they spoke; they sang; and then swiftly also they disappeared, leaving the night silent and empty again. One can imagine the shepherds sitting there spellbound about their camp fire. They are speechless with wonder, staring at each other, and yet scarcely seeing. At last one of them finds his voice, and exclaims: "Let us go even now to Bethlehem, and see this *word* which has become a fact, which the Lord has made known unto us."

They hear him, but even so his voice hardly breaks the spell which is upon them. At last they comprehend, and when they do, instantly, they are alert to go to Bethlehem. Swiftly climbing the steeper eastern approach to the city, and coming up on top of Bethlehem's hills, they see in the moonlight a solitary figure sitting at the entrance to one of the local limestone caves.

"Do you know where the newly born Child rests, who is Messiah and Saviour?" they ask.

"Why are you looking for such a wondrous Child?" the man responds.

"We have just seen a vision of angels," answer the shepherds. "They told us about him, and then they sang, 'Glory to God!'"

"The angels were right," said Joseph. "The Child has been born. He is inside this very grotto, lying in a manger."

Silently Joseph led the way within the cave and silently, also, the shepherds followed him, falling upon their knees in adoration.

So the night of Nativity passes, and then swiftly, too, it falls behind. Weeks intervene. Joseph has moved his family from the limestone grotto to one of Bethlehem's square limestone houses. Being a carpenter, he easily finds work in David's ancient city. He has already decided to remain there, and not take Mary back to Nazareth. It is now evening. Joseph's day's work is done, and he is at home with Mary. Chancing to look out upon the street, he sees a cavalcade stopping near. One of the camel drivers approaches his door. Yes, he knocks. Who can he be? What can he want?

Joseph opens. The man says to him, "Lords from the East have come to your city looking for a wondrous Child. He has recently been born king of the Jews. Can you tell us where we should look for him?"

"Are you indeed lords from the East?" Joseph inquired warily.

"We are, indeed," replied the stranger; "and we have traveled the long, long miles of the desert to render homage to this glorious Child. We saw His star in the East; and last night we saw it again hanging over this ancient city."

"Yes, I can tell you of this Child," said Joseph, "but one has to be careful. You men, however, are evidently what you say, so I will let you see the Child. This lady is His mother."

Immediately the men were on their knees; and then after a moment Mary went out and returned with the Child.

JESUS CHRIST IS LORD

The Wise Men gazed upon Him in reverent silence; and then one of them, addressing Mary, said, "Madam, may we present to Him our gifts?"

At first Mary was so astonished that she made no reply. Then quietly she said, "Yes, of course; but it is all so strange. I can hardly get accustomed to His greatness."

One by one, the men, rising from their knees, advanced and placed their gifts at her feet. There was gold, frankincense, and myrrh.

Then the audience ended; and the Wise Men, being warned of God in a dream, returned to the East without letting Herod know that they had found the wonderful Child.

That night as Joseph slept, God commanded him to flee immediately from Bethlehem, taking the Child and His mother with him into Egypt. The next morning he said to Mary, "I begin to understand it all now. King Herod is hostile to your glorious Child, and so we must flee with Him into Egypt. God warned me last night in a dream; and before that He sent to us these lords from the East with their gifts to meet our costs upon the journey."

So it was that Mary again rode the faithful ass, her Child resting upon her bosom. The second morning found her once again at the house of Elizabeth, for the road into Egypt passed by it. Before the week was out Joseph and his family had crossed the border. They were in Egypt, and the Child was safe from Herod's wild wrath.

Thus it was that Messiah was born 1960 years ago;

and thus it was that God kept Him safe from the futile wrath of men. "Why do the heathen rage . . . the kings of the earth set themselves, and the rulers take council together? . . . He that sitteth in the heavens shall laugh. The Lord shall have them in derision!" How easily God made Herod's wrath a useless barbarity nineteen hundred years ago! And how easily God will always defeat the wrath of wicked men when they conspire against His holy purposes! Wicked men only prosper while God tolerates them, making use of them for His own high ends. When this brief hour is spent, God summons them to judgment. It was so He dealt with Herod; and it is so He always deals with proud men whose crimes disfigure history.

A closing word with respect to Archbishop Usher's strange mistake. We are surprised that so great a scholar could have made the mistake he did. Nevertheless chronology is not the easy study it seems to be. We need to remember that Christian beginnings lay 1657 years behind, when the Archbishop undertook to achieve a Christian chronology. Every event up to the publication of the archbishop's book, *Annals of the Old Testament,* had been dated after the founding of Rome. It was in the year 2271 A.U. that Luther nailed his celebrated theses to the door of the Castle Church at Wittenberg. It was in the year 2404 A.U. that the Archbishop brought out his epoch-making work, replacing Roman time with Christian time. That book was probably the first writing dated by Christian chronology—1650 A.D. Consequently it was exceedingly easy even for a learned scholar to have made the mistake he did.

But quite apart from his mistake, his great insight was remarkable. He saw that Jesus Christ divided history; that all time before He came, was before the Lord; that all time since He came was within His era, and so under His blessing. So Rome was founded 747 before Christ came to illumine the world. The birth of Christ is the absolute date. It is relative to nothing. Everything is relative to it.

THE TRANSFIGURATION
St. Matthew 16:28

"Verily I say unto you, There be some standing here which shall not taste death till they see the Son of Man coming in his kingdom."

Jesus evidently looked upon the Transfiguration as a significant *coming* of the Son of Man; and this also was the point of view of the primitive Church. We see this quite definitely in a casual remark in the *Second Epistle of Peter,* where the Transfiguration is named a manifestation of the "power and coming of our Lord Jesus Christ" (1:16, 17). We see it also in the circumstance that all three of the synoptic gospels stand the Transfiguration in the context of Jesus' statement that some of the apostles will not taste death until they have seen Him coming in His Kingdom (St. Matt. 16:28f; St. Mark 9:1f; St. Luke 9:27f).

Jesus saw His Kingdom advancing through the influence of a slowly enlarging community of faith. The influence of this community would produce manifold social changes, and each important crisis in this advance would be a *coming*. The key verse which makes Jesus' point of view explicit is the sentence in which He answered the High Priest before the Sanhedrin. We will have occasion to deal with this sentence more fully later on, but even now we take time to point out that Jesus said (*ap arti*) *"From now on* ye shall see the Son of Man seated at the right hand of power, and coming in the clouds of heaven" (St. Matt. 26:64). *Ap arti* means "from now on"; and the translators who have rendered it by "hereafter" have probably done so to bring the Biblical expression into harmony with what they have understood to be Jesus' expectation. But Jesus' expectation was precisely as He expressed it. He saw Himself from His crucifixion and resurrection forward as evidently seated at the right hand of power, and *coming*. He saw every crisis of history as a manifestation of His authority and increase. "The Kingdom of God come in power", "The Son of man coming in His kingdom", and "The Son of Man seated at the right hand of power and coming in the clouds of heaven", were just three different ways of saying exactly the same thing.

Jesus, then, and the primitive Church which He taught regarded the Transfiguration as a *coming*. It was a powerful Divine self disclosure which marked off a stage within Jesus' incarnate ministry. It was in fact a heavenly fore-announcement of Christ's final glory, given both to Him and to the apostles, as He ended His preaching ministry, and began the approach to His passion.

Jesus may or may not have known in advance the precise nature of this heavenly disclosure. He knew that it would come, and that it would be given to some of the apostolic group to witness it. Six days intervened between Jesus' announcement and its fulfillment. (St. Luke says, "about eight days afterward"). The Saviour was with the apostles on Mount Hermon. He left the larger group on one of its lower elevations, and taking with Him, Peter, James, and John climbed higher for a season of communion with His Father.

Jesus' prayer effort on that occasion became lengthened, and His apostolic guard fell asleep. Then suddenly it happened. His appearance was changed. His face became luminous. His garments became exceeding white and glistening. The apostolic guard was wakened, and gazing upon His glory, they saw Moses and Elias appearing with Him and communing with Him about His forthgoing that He was about to accomplish at Jerusalem.

In view of the insights of the new physics, which have reduced all material things to appearances—mere phenomena—such a temporary change in the character of Jesus' physical body involves no problem. The pattern of any physical body can be changed by its Creator quite as easily as the patterns of figures on the moving picture screen can be changed by the operator. Those figures on the screen continuously take their particular shape as various beams of colored light stream from the projector. So Jesus' physical body was continuously taking its particular shape as cosmic forces streamed from the will of His Father. If then, the Father changed His creative purpose for some reason, the stream of forces which flowed from His creative will would be altered, and Jesus' physical body would be modified.

Evidently something approximating Jesus' body of the Resurrection was given to Him at the Transfiguration. And since St. Paul is explicit that Jesus was the first to be raised from the dead, something of the same approximation must have been given also to Moses and Elias. I am deeply impressed by this apostolic insight.

JESUS CHRIST IS LORD

It is completely fitting that the first introduction of Eternal Life into the universe should take place in connection with the glorious personality of the incarnate Son. So we must conceive of Jesus as "clothed upon" at the Transfiguration, and Moses and Elias as specially clothed for the occasion. Each of these three, then, was made outwardly manifest in bodies of glory. They saw themselves. They saw each other; and they were seen by the apostles.

It is not surprising that the conversation of that august moment was concerned with Jesus' forthgoing—His exodus which He was about to accomplish at Jerusalem. That stupendous Divine sacrifice was the absorbing concern of all heaven. The Son of God had identified Himself with sinners, and was about to accept the bitter pain which man's proud malice chose to thrust upon Him. Of course God, angels, and all victorious spirits would regard such a sacrifice with consuming interest.

Strikingly enough the heavenly visitants seemed to avoid the familiar word for human death in their communion. They spoke rather of His exodus, His forthgoing. There is a most beautiful suggestiveness in this choice of words. Moses and Elias, with their heavenly point of view, would naturally look upon Jesus' death as a forthgoing. He was indeed going away from earth; but He was going into the glory of God. He was going, as He said, to prepare a place for those whom He loved. He was immediately coming again; and then, after a time, He would receive them into His glorified presence. With this total vision in mind, Moses and Elias would hardly make use of the ordinary word for "death". No, it was definitely a forthgoing they were contemplating on the mount of the Transfiguration.

And now we come specifically to the central question: Why the Transfiguration?

Of course it was, as we already have noted, Heaven's particular accrediting of Jesus as He began His more definite approach to the Cross. But why did Jesus need this accrediting? And why did the apostles need to experience Him thus glorified?

The Gospels do not explicitly answer this question; but an explicit answer hardly seems necessary. Such an accrediting belonged to Jesus; and it was both the Father's joy and obligation to give it. God forever rejoices to do that which is fitting; and certainly no event of history was ever more fitting than that which momentarily lifted the incarnate Son into a foretaste of the eternal glory before He advanced into the extreme humiliation and bitterness of the Cross.

Jesus' acceptance of the Cross was a real and a costly moral decision. He chose it, indeed, with moral enthusiasm, but He chose it none the less in extreme sacrifice. We get some advance understanding of the severity of the choice of the Cross from St. Luke's record "that Jesus set his face to go to Jerusalem" (9:51). Jesus' choice of the Cross was consequently a strongly determined purpose. It was something that He powerfully willed. The account of the agony in Gethsemane gives us a very much deeper understanding of the terrific effort involved.

The Cross is a paradox. It is something dreadfully

false, which becomes something infinitely true because God has accepted it into His glory in love and hope. As a human being Jesus felt the horror and humiliation of the cross; but as the Son of God in perfect fellowship with His Father, Jesus felt also the perfect Truth of the *Cross*. This high experience, however, characterized only the Saviour's experience of full personality. It was when He deeply knew Himself that He deeply knew also His Father, and felt the beauty of His purpose in His acceptance of the *Cross*. When, however, He dropped below the level of this high self grasp, He felt only natural human emotions, and saw the cross in its inherent horror and humiliation.

Any one who has carefully observed his own experiences is familiar with this distinction between personal and sub-personal attitudes. Some men are timid and shrinking at the sub-personal level, and completely fearless at the personal level. Others are narrowly selfish at the sub-personal level, and understanding and generous at the personal level. At the sub-personal level behavioristic psychology is true. At the personal level a completely new force has been released into the situation. It is the force of creative, self-decisive action; and it often discloses an attitude completely the reverse of the mere natural reactions of an individual.

When Jesus was in the Upper Room, He was fully personal. He was experiencing full self-grasp, and unbounded fellowship with His Father. Consequently when the betrayer went out to consummate his perfidy, Jesus exclaimed, "Now is the Son of Man glorified, and

God is glorified in him." But as the evening wore on with Jesus steadily living at this nervously exacting level, He became weary, and the period of His ascent from mere individuality into personality became markedly lengthened. If at the beginning of the evening this reaction time was the one-hundredth part of a second, at the end of the evening it might have been as long as half a second, or even a second. Consequently at the end of the evening Jesus felt the horror of the cross as a mere human experience definitely before He felt it sublimated into the *Cross* by His humble redemptive acceptance of it.

Here is the explanation of that apparent lack of constantcy characteristic of Jesus' expressions in Gethsemane. He began His prayer at the sub-personal level. He was a mere individual. The effort of prayer, however, immediately lifted Him into full personality, at which level He saw again the whole sweep of His Father's purpose. The begining of each petition was thus His expression of a tired individual's reaction to the horror of the cross; but during the half second that it took to express this emotion, He rose into full personality. Living in the reaches of meaning this experience opened to Him, He both saw anew, and chose the *Cross*.

The point I am making is that Jesus' choice of the *Cross* was an actual personal effort, a costly moral victory. Jesus chose the Cross, and He chose it against the uninterrupted pressure of all His natural reactions. Manifestly the eternal Father would want to give His Son every possible support and recognition as He moved into this terrific effort. The Transfiguration was the Father's support and recognition. It was given both to Jesus and to the Twelve as the shadow of Calvary became a near and dominant reality.

It is interesting to note that God uniformly gives His servants these experiences of support and recognition as they draw near to the crises of their lives. St. Paul calls attention to a number of visions accorded to him as his hour of martyrdom came nearer. He speaks of being caught up into the third heaven, and of experiencing revelations unspeakable (II Cor. 12:2); and St. Luke records two other visions which were given to him much nearer the end of his career—one when he was arrested at Jerusalem (Acts 23:11), and one when he was in imminent peril during the great storm (Acts 27:23).

God, then, does always give His servants the recognition and support which they need to cooperate in His glorious purposes. The Divine gift is always enough to inspire a free response, but never enough to go beyond inspiration and become coercive. The creature's free responses are sacred to God; and He never allows His glorious disclosures to be powerful enough to replace them with coercions.

The Transfiguration, then, was a recognition given to Jesus and to the apostles as they drew near to the exacting strain of Good Friday. Realizing all the resources which God had made available to the Twelve, we would marvel at the failure of their faith if we did not know how very weak and forgetful human nature constantly tends to be. We men and women so easily lose sight of our former deliverances when confronted by some new danger. It takes real character effectively to remember the glory of yesterday amid the oppressive darkness of today.

Confront the resources God had provided to establish the faith of the Twelve! They had their three years of contact with the elevated life of Jesus. They had their recollections of His mighty works. They had the glory of the Transfiguration with the heavenly voice which confessed Him. They had His own repeated prophecies of the Cross and of the Resurrection which would follow it. It was an immense equipment, and they should have stood even through Good Friday, but they did not; and they did not because they failed to make the response of that strongly purposed faith God had the right to expect of them.

It is important to emphasize the necessity for this human response. The character and history of a son are not sovereign works of God, but a cooperative accomplishment, involving the creative willing of the creature as well as of the Creator. And God will never allow any costliness of the possible consequences to exclude the creature's opportunity for creative purposing. This is one of the deepest principles of probationary time, and God's regard for it is absolute.

It was under the government of this principle that the incarnate Son of God carefully limited His mighty works, and often commanded the recipients of His grace to be silent about their benefits. Thus, He could heal the sick, and even raise the dead; but He could not climb to the pinnacle of the Temple and leap boldly

JESUS CHRIST IS LORD

into space, depending upon the omnipotence of His Father to enable Him to alight safely in the Temple courts. Such a spectacular miracle would have been coercive to faith, and would not have left room for free, creative, moral purposing in the believer.

We are making a most important distinction. Jesus both sought and even waited for the believing responses of men. He urged them to believe Him because of the total impact of His life upon them, adding, If you are not equal to this high opportunity, and cannot believe me for myself, then believe me for the work's sake (St. John 14:11). Doubtless the New Testament's concentration of miracles is the most abundant in history. It far surpasses anything in the Old Testament: but when you consider the inherent possibilities of the Incarnation, it is scanty notwithstanding.

It is probable Peter, James and John observed that silence with respect to the Transfiguration Jesus commanded; but after the Resurrection they were released from all restraint, and immediately imparted to the Twelve the immense truths it had disclosed. There are two facts which make it certain that the Transfiguration was regarded as a most important revelation by the apostolic group. The first is that it is so spoken of in the Second Epistle of Peter. The second is that the three synoptic evangelists, no one of whom shared the experience, all narrate it, and even with marked agreement as to its details. Indeed, St. Matthew and St. Luke, who are usually dependent upon St. Mark for their narrative sections, are clearly not dependent upon him here, for their accounts of the event are considerably richer than St. Mark's. The easiest explanation of this striking circumstance is that the Transfiguration with its most significant disclosures was so prominently discussed in the primitive Church that its details were common property. We can understand this, because the witness to the Cross by Moses and Elias, and the witness to Jesus by the heavenly Voice must have provided the Twelve with a secure foundation when they began the difficult task of putting into language the wonder of their experience of Jesus. The Resurrection experience had burst all the familiar categories they had known within the tradition of Abraham and Moses. The words of the heavenly Voice connected with the Transfiguration came just in time to provide them with a new category. Jesus was God's Son. He was One transcendently close to God, who both revealed and obeyed Him.

The Transfiguration has, thus, a four fold significance:

(1) It is an advance recognition given both to Jesus and to the Twelve as He enters more intimately upon the way of the Cross.

(2) It is a revelation of Jesus' eternal glory given to the apostles to help them conceive the unique significance of His person.

(3) It is the first in a long series of *comings* through which the infant Kingdom would be expanded until at last it realized the ancient promise of the prophetic age of peace.

(4) Then beyond all these intermediate *comings*,

there would at last be the *Coming,* in which the glory which had been merely prophetic at the Transfiguration, would be completely realized.

THE TRIUMPHAL ENTRY

St. John 12:17-18

"The people, therefore, which were with Him when He called Lazarus out of his grave, and raised him from the dead, bare record. For this cause the people also met Him, for they had heard that He had done this miracle."

The Triumphal Entry is one of history's most dramatic events. It is Jesus' final summons to the Israel of His day, and sacred history's prophecy of the Saviour's ultimate universal sovereignty.

Standing at the threshold of this climax, one's mind inevitably surveys the succession of great events which lie immediately behind it.

The Star, the Virgin mother, and the Manger!

The Baptism with its opening sky, and its mighty voice!

The short Judaean ministry which ended just before the imprisonment of John the Baptist!

The longer Galileean ministry with its miracles, its sermons, and its parables!

The approach to the Cross, which included the exalted spectacle of the Transfiguration and the supreme miracle of the raising of Lazarus from the dead!

What a succession of happenings!

Our present story opens with the last of them—Jesus' raising from the dead a man four days buried, in whose mortal remains disintegration had already set in.

JESUS CHRIST IS LORD

The story is told in St. John alone; and the reason is evident—Lazarus was now a second time dead, and there was no longer reason to suppress the story out of fear of the rulers, who at the beginning had considered putting Lazarus to death (St. John 12:10). After the destruction of Jerusalem this fear passed; and the circumstance that no account of Jesus' supreme miracle appears in the synoptic gospels is an added reason for dating all three of those writings before that epoch-making event.

When Jesus in Peraea received the news that Lazarus was seriously sick, He said: "This sickness is not unto death, but for the glory of God, that the Son of God may be glorified." Four days later He was standing beside Mary and Martha at their brother's sealed tomb. The situation was completely hopeless. Lazarus' body had been in its sepulchre four days, and disintegration had already begun. Jesus, however, was serene, confident. As if oblivious to the circumstances, He commanded the sealing stone to be removed from the mouth of the sepulchre. Martha exclaimed in shocked protest, but Jesus insisted. The stone was removed; and amid the odor of decomposition which freighted the air, Jesus breathed a prayer of thanksgiving: "Father I thank thee that thou hast heard me." Then followed the clear resonant command, which spectators about the tomb called, "a loud voice"—"Lazarus, come forth!"

This was the supreme miracle of Jesus' incarnate life. There was no possibility either of calling it in question, or of explaining it away. The only course now open to the enemies of Jesus was to destroy both Him and Lazarus, and hope that the people would forget before the event had produced too great consequences. This course, however, could not immediately be put in operation, for Jesus had disappeared into the wilderness, and they did not know where to find Him. Manifestly the killing of Lazarus apart from the killing of Jesus had no significance whatever. Consequently, the rulers did nothing for the moment, and while they waited the story of this great miracle stirred the countryside.

Now it was the time of the annual Passover Pilgrimage, and the people began their ascent to Jerusalem. The crowd was large, for the story of the raising of Lazarus had been whispered everywhere, and there was great popular interest. People thought Jesus would probably come to the feast; and so they came hoping to see Him, and perhaps to see Lazarus also.

Then quite suddenly Jesus appeared. He was seen one day walking among the pilgrims going up to the feast. Instantly He was the center of attention. There was great conversation about Him, and many sought His help along the road. Mothers wanted Him to bless their babies. Blind men clamored to have their sight restored. A rich young ruler knelt to Him, asking for the solution of life. I have long entertained the idea that this young ruler was Saul of Tarsus who afterward became St. Paul.

The Songs of the Ascent which the pilgrims sang had a new lilt that year—how very glad they were to be going up to the House of the Lord! High expecta-

JESUS CHRIST IS LORD

tion was in the air. Was this new prophet the Messiah? Who else could He be, performing such miracles?

The Sabbath Day found Jesus in Bethany; and in the evening after the sun had set they staged a great feast for Him—a feast for Jesus and Lazarus! The excitement was high; and the next day Jesus organized it into a dramatic expression. Zechariah had long ago prophesied that the Messianic King would ride into Jerusalem upon the poor man's beast rather than upon the royal mule (9:9), and now Jesus deliberately plans to fulfill the prediction—He rides into Jerusalem upon an ass.

It must have been about noon on Sunday when the disciples bring to Jesus the colt, and placing their abbas upon its back for a saddle, seat Jesus thereon. The meaning of the act is instantly clear. Prophecy is being fulfilled. Some one raises the shout, "Hosanna to the Son of David!" and immediately a hundred voices make answer. The pilgrims carpet the road with their abbas. They strip branches from the palm trees and lay these upon the road. So singing, shouting, waving palms, they surround Jesus as He begins His coronation approach to Jerusalem.

But now we must pause for a moment to refresh our recollections with respect to the topography of that section. Jerusalem is built upon a cluster of hills; and these are separated from another cluster of even higher hills by the narrow valley of the Kedron. There is a point on the road approaching Jerusalem from Bethany where the city bursts suddenly into view, and lies there gleaming white across the narrow valley. At this point there is, of course, a great shout from the pilgrim crowd: "Hosanna to the Son of David! Blessed is he that cometh in the name of the Lord!"

Jesus, however, seems not to share the excited mood of the crowd. He halts His little beast as the city bursts into view, and sits there gazing upon it. He says something; and those who are near enough hear the words of a lament, and see tears coursing down His cheeks: "O Jerusalem, if thou hadst known, even thou, at least in this thy day, the things that belong to thy peace! but now they are hid from thine eyes" (St. Luke 19:41).

The enthusiasm, however, of the crowd is too great to be chilled by the Saviour's tears. There is only a momentary pause; and soon their lilting songs are echoing again across the valley. In the city the people hear and make answer to the shout from the mountain. Quickly, without any one organizing it, a procession takes form in the city and moves eastward through the gates and over the Kedron. The singing is now antiphonal. The two groups are moving toward each other. In a matter of moments they meet on the slope of Olivet. The excitement is indescribable. Even the children feel it, and their high pitched voices punctuate the louder shouts of their elders. Singing and shouting the procession at last enters the Holy City. They crowd through the gates, and move on into the Temple courts.

Jesus contemplates the great spectacle—the sacred buildings, the excited multitude, the little groups of rulers and pharisees moving in angry silence through it or on its fringes. Then after a time the shouting dies down. Nothing happens, and the crowd is weary of shouting. It has never entered into their minds to repent of their sins; and Jesus has quite no thought of accepting any other recognition of His Messiahship. And so nothing happens; and the great demonstration comes to an end. After an infinite moment in which a thousand things could have been done, and nothing was done, Jesus leaves the Temple and makes His solitary way out over the Kedron, and back to Bethany. Jesus is king no longer. He could not be the king they wanted. They could not recognize Him as the King He was.

The futile ending of that excited demonstration strikes one with the solemnity of judgment day. There had been no meeting of minds. There existed no unity of wills. Jerusalem's people could think profoundly enough to conceive an Incarnation, but they could not think existentially enough to know how to behave in the Incarnate presence. They were lacking in moral reality. And so a tremendous hour dawned, unfolded, and passed, and nothing happened. A great crowd had shouted "Hosanna!" to a king who was not, and had completely failed to discern the King who was.

All that is now two thousand years behind us; and a new civilization is once again standing in another hour of crisis and destiny. In part, too, we comprehend our situation as poorly as the Jerusalem crowd did theirs, two thousand years ago. We weave our natural-

---

* The author fully recognizes the importance of academic freedom; but with every fundamental truth and dignity of life hanging in the balance, one cannot avoid the feeling that some of those who magnify it are lacking in the moral earnestness necessary to existential thought.

istic speculations. We are excited about academic freedom*; and there is only one thing big enough to be excited about—the grandeur of our free moral personalities, and the response we ought to make to the holy God! God has been seeking us all the way from Abraham to Jesus, in the Resurrection, through the Church, through our democratic institutions—the dignity of Christian manhood clothed for political action. Yes, what response ought we to make to this holy God? The things that have happened in our day are as unescapable, and as challenging as the ancient raising of Lazarus from the dead. We are living in the atomic age. Our world has been condensed into a congested neighborhood. We are not dying animals or helpless automata, but majestic moral personalities facing the sheer wonder of the fact of Christ. And as we stand thus confronting Him new scribes and pharisees move angrily among us—exponents of Naturalism, Scientific Determinism, Behaviorism, Secularism, Communism. The question of the hour is what do we mean to do about this challenge? Merely singing "God Bless America" and saluting the flag are a no more significant response than shouting "Hosanna to the Son of David" was two thousand years ago! The holy God with whom we have to do is interested now, as He was then, with repentance, faith, the service of truth, devoted living, Christian witnessing.

If the great leaders of our day were Hebrew prophets, they would be shouting to us about a day of judgment—a Day of Jehovah—for this is an hour of crisis and decision. One can appreciate Elton True-

JESUS CHRIST IS LORD   65

blood's appeal to Christian men to make the service of Christ a second vocation. One can understand Arnold Toynbee's volume *Democracy on Trial*. Large faith, high moral purpose, a new intellectual seriousness, a new appreciation of the moral dignity of personality, a new humble glory at the supreme grandeur of Jesus—this is the attitude that can meet the crisis of our times. The Martyr Church some seventeen hundred years ago gave us the cry that our age now again needs to lift, JESUS CHRIST IS LORD! Lord of our minds, Lord of our emotions, Lord of our day by day living: and when some millions of us lift this cry, and mean this commitment, both life and civilization will advance magnificently.

The other truth: Palm Sunday was prophetic. It was very much more than the colossal failure it has seemed just as it took place in history. In Israel's long experience a great many events have a double significance. They are happenings at some ancient time, long ago, and they are prophecies looking far toward the future. So Abraham's sacrifice of Isaac was typical of God's sacrifice of His only begotten Son. So David's conquests in Palestine were typical of Messiah's increasing Kingdom. So Solomon's broad recognition was typical of Messiah's universal sway. And just so, too, Palm Sunday's acclaim of Jesus was prophetic of the day when He will be acclaimed as King of kings and Lord of lords.

And how like the ancient Palm Sunday this day will be! Jesus will descend the skies surrounded by the victors who have been reigning with Him above history. And then the saints on earth, like men of ancient Jerusalem, will ascend to meet Him as He descends. The two companies will meet, the two great halleluiahs will blend. The rapture of this acclaim will sweep all opposition from before it. It will divide men right and left, as a shepherd divideth the sheep from the goats. And then the shout for which history has long been waiting will reverberate through the universe—"Halleluiah! Halleluiah! The kingdom of this world is become the Kingdom of our Lord and of His Christ; and He shall reign forever and forever, King of kings and Lord of lords—Halleluiah!"

THE CROSS—God so loved.

St. John 3:16

"God so loved the world that he gave his only begotten Son, that whosoever believeth in him should not perish, but have everlasting life."

"God so loved the world!" Just to say, "God loved the world" is sublime; but to say, "Go *so* loved the world" is infinite. The "so" of the Gospels is an adverb of exact comparison, and the sentence could be rendered, "God loved the world in just this way." That which God did, consequently, discriminates the exact quality of God's love as well as the boundlessness of its intensity.

What, then, is the particular way in which God loved the world? The answer, of course, is, that He loved it in moral hope; that is He loved it as one who was disappointed with the world as it had been, and was willing to make immense sacrifices to make it what He longed that it should be.

Love is not an ultimate idea. It is a resultant depending upon other values which, operating behind it, produce it. Thus, love is sometimes grounded in a common moral concern; and this is the moral love of God. But sometimes love is grounded in a common appreciation of the beautiful; and this is the love of romance. Any common interest can be the spring of love. W love some other one because we are conscious of some large fellowship with that other one. Family love is grounded in common memories. The soldier's love for his comrade is grounded in common dangers and sacrifices.

Love at its best, however, is always grounded in a common moral concern; and all such love is called *moral love*. When such love discovers a great moral concern in its object, it experiences blessedness; and could properly be called *beatifying love*. But when moral love discovers no corresponding moral concern in its object, it loves only in hope, and should be called *redemptive love*. This is the love of God for sinful men. This also is the love of parents for their wayward children. They love those children in spite of what they are, and because of what they can become. Because they can become something different and nobler, the parent not only loves them in hope, but he gives himself to them in sacrifice to help them realize that nobler possibility. This is the redemptive love of God in Christ. It is not a beatifying love, but a sacrificial love. It is love which accepts immense cost to realize in his beloved the moral ideal he has for him.

There is one more possibility that love can discover. It is the attitude it develops when moral hope becomes exhausted, and the moral lover is compelled to recognize that he for whom he has hoped and sacrificed has committed himself completely to evil. When moral love discovers this hopeless finality it is changed into wrath. This is *The Revelation's* solemn truth of the wrath of God and the Lamb—the wrath of rejected redemptive love.

All these responses of personality are immediate and necessary. They are values belonging to God's eternal truth. They are as unescapable as the consequences that two times two are four, or that a valley is constituted by surrounding a depressed area with hills. God does not choose these principles of His truth, and God does not choose these responses of His moral love. God necessarily loves all holy personalities with beautifying joy; all sinning personalities, for whom there is yet hope, with redemptive self-sacrifice; all defiant personalities, who have committed themselves to evil, with a flame that has been transformed from love to wrath.

Scripture contains no suggestion that God has any hope for the salvation of those demonic personalities who in proud defiance resent His love. There is a proud self-assertion that hates both moral love and moral sacrifice. God's necessary response to such is a finality of judgment. But for sinful men, who are only learning the meaning of the great moral ideas, and who are as much confused as sinning, God does have hope; and the Bible is the record of the self-disclosures God has made, and the sacrificial toil He has accepted to accomplish man's salvation.

We move on, now from these important primary ideas, to a deeper appreciation of the holy God. God is not only a great moral tri-unity, who is both one and blessed because He is holy; but God is also a poet, an artist. He rejoices not only to be what He forever is, but also to express what He is, and to find the glory of His eternal life in abounding expression about Him. The universe, consequently, is related to God as a poem is related to its author. God is one, and the universe also is one. God is free, and the universe is at least moving up toward freedom. God is holy, and if the universe is not holy, still God has dedicated His utmost resource to make it so.

We have already seen that blessedness arises in holiness. Moral concern meeting moral concern in another necessarily loves and is beatified. It is, thus, completely impossible for God to make bad men blessed except by making them holy. It is not that God objects to bad men being blessed; it is that blessedness is profoundly impossible to them. Two times two simply cannot be a million; and it is just as impossible for pride and self-assertion to experience beatification. Humility has first to replace pride, and obedience to replace self-assertion. Then moral concern can appear, and unity can replace division. There is no other approach to blessedness; everlasting truth completely bars those other illusory approaches. God we must remember is limited at once by His truth, His holiness, and His purposes already projected. Consequently there are numbers of things that He is completely incapable of doing. God is not philosophy's unconditioned absolute; He is an infinite moral personality. When, therefore, God undertook to crown His cosmic poem with a free, holy, human society, He found Himself confronting certain necessary realities. He had to make man moral. He had to make man free; and He had to accept the risk that free man might make choice of proud self-assertion instead of humility and obedience.

God accepted the risk; and free man actually repudiated the humility and obedience by which alone he could complete God's cosmic poem and attain to his own fulfillment. The result was a tremendous and enduring falsehood projected by man both into life and into enduring history. Confronting this falsehood, God had to do something, for the universe no longer expressed Him. You might illustrate the tragic falsity of life and history because of sin, by imagining some one's having defaced Handel's "Halleluiah Chorus" with multiplied discords. In such a situation the musician would have to do something to save the truth of his chorus, and so also God had to do something to save the truth of His cosmic poem.

What can God do? The immediate answer is, of course, God can judge sin, standing judgment over against it in history, and so reversing its falsehood. Sin unjudged, is, of course, a lie; but sin judged becomes a negative expression of the truth. Thus murder unjudged mocks the sanctity of personality; but murder judged reaffirms that sanctity. Similarly sin in history mocks the holiness of God; but sin in history shut up to the futility of natural death, reaffirms, at least negatively, God's holiness. It does this by pointing out that proud, assertive man has missed the goal of his being, and that nature itself dooms him, in spite of his potentialities, to die just as rats and rattlesnakes do.

God, thus, by judgment, made a beginning in His program of salvation. Man had been created in part transcendent to nature, that is he had been created moral, aspiring, free, and with an impress of the infinite upon him. As one who had chosen sinful self-assertion, man's transcendence lost its meaning. He had turned his back on the fellowship of God, and as a consequence, unending life ceased to have value. The result was that God responding to man's sin, thrust him back within the limitations of nature. In doing this God judged man's sin, and caused the universe once again to speak true.

The value of this solemn judgment can be felt even by sinful men, for notwithstanding we are sinners ourselves, we rejoice when the monsters of history have died. If such men did not die, it would project such moral despair into life as would make a moral civilization impossible. Notwithstanding, then, the judgment of death upon sin overwhelms the rest of us also, the fact that it does overwhelm the monsters of history, renders a saving service to truth in all of our experiences, and more abundantly so in the experience of the holy God.

This universal judgment upon sin was God's beginning in salvation; but it never satisfied Him; and it did not satisfy Him for three reasons.

First, it left unexpressed His motive of love in moral hope which he felt for sinners.

Second, it surrendered man to tragic disappointment and doom—the only possibility open to him as a self-centered, self-assertive being.

Third, it left God's cosmic poem incomplete—the universe would never fully express the holy glory of God.

Because the judgment of natural death did so profoundly dissatisfy God, He had to do something about it. He had to preserve His emphasis upon judgment; and yet also, He had to rescue man from the tragedy his sin had brought upon him.

This double work God accomplished by accepting into His own life the bitter fruitage of man's proud self-assertion. The cross was the fruit of human sin. God accepted it in His incarnate life, and by the resurrection lifted it up into His glory. Man's sin had hated and crucified the perfect beauty of God. To act in this bitter way was sin's nature; and to express thus vividly sin's characteristic drive, was judgment upon it.

God and all holy personalities necessarily felt the solemn majesty of this juxtaposition between human sin and Divine suffering. Sin's inherent nature and falsity was cosmically proclaimed. No holy personality could ever confront any sinful act without feeling the enormity of what it had done to God.

The fact that God had freely accepted this in moral love for the sinner's sake, made it not only an effective vicarious judgment, but also a tremendous expression of His infinite redemptive love. Immediately the reality of his self-sacrifice became known, the cross became the *Cross,* and men had to know that the holy God loved sinful probationary man, notwithstanding His first expression had been one of blasting judgment.

But it is not only God and holy personalities who face the reality of this immense sacrifice; demons and probationary sinners also face the same. Demons will know the cross for what it is, the *Cross;* but probationary sinners will be confronted by an uncertainty, a probability, and a choice. If the moral glory of Jesus,

Easter morning's empty tomb, and the victorious witness of the apostles to Jesus' resurrection are accepted at their face value, then sinners will be powerfully challenged. They will be summoned to repentance. This summons, however, will not be coercive. Sinners will still have a choice. They will be able to yield their pride in self-denial, or to stiffen it in even stronger self-assertion.

If they make the first choice, the cross will become the *Cross* for them, even as it is for God. It will express a solemn, infinite judgment on all the self-centeredness that life has been. In this experience of repentance the sinner will die unto self; and beyond it, he will live only by faith in the sheer wonder of God's holy love.

If, however, sinners choose to make the second choice, the cross will remain just the cross; and the sinner's pride and self-assertion will harden toward that complete defiance of God, which is the maturity of sin.

One of the robbers who was crucified beside Jesus chose the first of these possibilities. He confessed that the cross was the fit reward of his evil deeds, and he fixed his hope outside himself in the kingly nobility of Jesus.

The other robber chose the second possibility. He magnified his pride, mocking Jesus to appear sporting to the crowd. He was indeed up against it; but he would mock the one-time prophet and miracle worker along with the rest.

Let us seek now to come closer to this tremendous

JESUS CHRIST IS LORD

act and expression of God.

First, *judgment* is a very different thing from *penalty*. Judgment is moral self-expression set over against sin. *Penalty* is one particular form of moral self-expression—that form in which the sinner endures an experience of condemnatory suffering. *Penalty* is not necessary to foreginess. *Judgment* is.

Second, the law of *judgment* is that the expression of condemnation must be stood intimately over against the sin it condemns. It must be stood so emotionally near that sin that the memory of the sin, and of the judgment in which it is condemned will be one recollection.

Third, when the Holy God confronts human sin and His expression of judgment upon it in the Cross, He realizes that He is perfectly expressed. Everything that He feels both of judgment and of love is fully uttered; and so He forgives freely—to the uttermost. This is the amazing sufficiency of God's redemptive love. It is as moral as judgment. It is as gracious as literally unbounded self-giving can be.

Fourth, when the repentant sinner, seeing thus the *Cross*, comprehends the falsity of his proud assertions, he dies to his former self-centeredness, and lives only by faith in the all-sufficiency and love of God.

Confront, now, the events of that Good Friday-Easter morning weekend of the year 30. The Gospels say there was an earthquake, a military guard placed at the tomb, the vision of an angel, a terrified prostration of soldiers, the Roman seal was broken, the Saviour's tomb was open. The average residents of Jerusalem, of course, came in contact with these events only indirectly, or partially. The earthquake was generally known. The terror of the soldiers was widely whispered. The open empty sepulchre was an indisputable fact. The bold witness of the apostles was as widely known, and almost as challenging. Inevitably men asked themselves: Who was He? Is He really risen from the dead? What did we and our rulers do when we crucified Him? Gamaliel, who confronted the Sanhedrin with something approximating these queries was far from being the only person in Jerusalem who was asking them (Acts 5:38, 39).

And so the cross became *the Cross*. During probationary time of course, there will always have to be the cooperating choice of the repentant sinner to complete the change; but when that cooperating choice is made, the Spirit will reveal the eternal meaning of Good Friday and Easter morning with saving power. Men will see in them the death of One who did not have to die. They will see in them their own proud malice thrusting a bitter cross on One before whom they should rather have bowed in worship. Because their pride had made them incapable of understanding Him, they scourged Him. Because He loved them still, and turned the other cheek, they crucified Him.

Such arrogance of course is sin—an expression of sin's bitter self-centeredness. Because God accepted it, humbly, faithfully, and in love, He made it also an expression of His utter devotion to probationary sinners. Because it was the everlasting Righteousness which suffered this pain, that Righteousness with

which man must always have to do, the suffering of the Cross becomes not only an expression of sin and of love, but also of judgment—judgment vicariously born. Because all this history was at the Ascension lifted up into the eternal glory, it became the everlasting forth-utterance of God's holiness come in contact with probationary sin, and so the perfect mediator of salvation. This is the Cross of Christ—
The eternal symbol of sin!
The eternal symbol of judgment!
The eternal symbol of unbounded moral love!
God thus makes of Himself a gazing stock set in the very midst of the universe and of the ages; and as men come into self-denying, humble, believing contact with Him they are transformed.

Of course these depths and reaches of truth were not manifest on Golgotha that Good Friday; but they began to be manifest on Easter morning; and from that moment forward the Spirit of God by this history has been wooing proud, assertive, sinful men.

The Cross is thus not something God thrust upon His Son. The cross was man conceived, but God accepted. Jesus the Son of God freely accepted it and loved man through the whole bitter experience. When hanging in agony upon Golgotha Jesus prayed for those who were deriding Him, He achieved such an expression of Moral Truth as no malice can possibly misconceive, and no flight of the centuries can ever make irrelevant.

The philosophy behind Jesus' magnificent expression is that which He Himself announced when He called men to turn the other cheek (Matt. 5:39). He meant that love must remain faithful even in spite of the bitterness of blows. Moral love must both judge sinners and love sinners until all possibility of redemption is exhausted. Jesus taught this, and then also He lived it: and He lived it as one who stood so close to God that His love was God's love, and His pain was an expression of God's long self-sacrifice.

During probationary time, as we have already pointed out, something of interpretation is necessary as men face these Divine acts. Men confront the events and choose. Their choices are basic moral decisions. The repentant choice progressively abolishes pride. The proud choice progressively abolishes sincerity. We see the first decision in St. Paul, whose life had room for no other glory save only the love of God in the Cross. We see the second decision in Caiaphas, who after the Resurrection, proudly extended his malice beyond Jesus to His followers.

When men make the first choice, they unite with God in lifting up the Cross to the place of supreme significance in history. They unite with God in making it a cosmic expression at once of sin, of judgment, and of love.

When men make the second choice, they unite with Caiaphas in obscuring the grace of God, and transform the infinite Cross into a mere meaningless and tragic spectacle.

It is of course impossible to find within history a complete analogy of this Divine act of moral self-sacrifice. However, Abraham Lincoln's mood in the

Second Inaugural does approximate it. The martyred President had in those days a fairly definite feeling that his own death had to be stood in history as a kind of concluding sacrifice to all the sacrifices of the Civil War; and he had said to one or two friends, "If such is God's will, I am ready." Lincoln may, and he may not have realized that such a sacrifice would reveal to a multitude North and South the dreadful wrongness of the war, and the love that had accepted the war rather than surrender the Union. I do not know Lincoln's precise thought about his sacrifice when he said, "I am ready"; but I do know Jesus' thought about His; and it was precisely to **reveal man's sin, to reveal** God love, and to stand vicarious judgment in history in such a tremendous way as to make the judgment of natural death no longer a **Divine necessity.**

The Cross is thus the nexus of all moral relationships. It is an eternal expression at once of sin, of judgment upon sin, and of God's redemptive love toward sinners that makes possible a satisfying moral forgiveness. God, now, can forgive all sinners because He deeply feels that everything He forever means about righteousness, about sin, and about confused frustrated sinners is in perfect expression. And not only can God forgive all sinners, but sinners can forgive each other, and they can even forgive themselves as they feel themselves forever standing in the context of this infinite expression.

What is the moral necessity of a great act of forgiveness? It is to have lifted up in the context of the sin such an expression of condemnation upon sin, and such an expression of love for the sinner as will make totally clear everything that each moral personality feels. This is what God needs. This is what all holy personalities need. This is what even the sinner needs if his acceptance of the grace of God is to be morally satisfying. His self-denying repentance must be fully in expression. Every man who looks at him must see his appreciation of the Cross in his face. When you stand beside the sea, you always hear an undertone of the sea, no matter what else you are hearing: and so in the forgiven sinner there must be always an appreciation of the Cross sounding through everything else that he does or says. Every saved sinner is thus a man who has died and been made alive again in relation to the Cross. He has died unto pride, independence, self-assertion; and he has been made alive unto humility, trust, and obedience. He is Christ enriched, Christ empowered, and Christ guaranteed. St. Paul put it vividly when he exclaimed, "I am crucified with Christ; yet I live; but not I, Christ lives in me" (Galatians 2:20).

In this tremendous experience the former lost sinner is inwardly transformed into a saint. He has become one who has attained to live by the law of God's life, and so to experience the rapture of God's blessedness. The ancient covenant of Abraham is fulfilled in him. He lives in the Divine presence; and his every act and expression is inspired by the wonder and wisdom of the Divine fellowship.

Here is a deeply moral story, which comes nearer to providing an analogy for the Cross than any other

JESUS CHRIST IS LORD

of which I have knowledge. In a certain New Jersey village, forty odd years ago, there lived a plumber, his wife, and his child—David, a boy of five or six years. The plumber was a man of violent temper, who was shockingly profane. David was a member of the Methodist Sunday School, and the plumber occasionally came to church in the evening.

One day this man's windmill broke, and after some delay he determined to repair it. He brought his tallest ladder, and stood it against the frame of his windmill. He was disappointed, for it did not reach the point where the windmill was broken by three feet. The plumber, however, would not be diverted from his purpose, so he determined to lengthen his ladder by the dangerous expedient of setting it upon the foundation of a large packing box, which had long stood upon his back porch.

Having brought the box, and erected the ladder upon it, the plumber was gratified to notice that it now reached beyond the broken part. He carefully shook the ladder, and noticed that both it and the box seemed firm. Consequently, gathering up some bolts and wrenches, he ascended.

Reaching the broken part, he worked upon it for several minutes. The repair was nearly complete; but he found he could not finish it without another wrench. Since little David was playing on the ground not far away, the plumber called down to him to get the wrench he needed and bring it up the ladder. For some reason David was slow to obey. Then immediately the plumber was in a rage. He cursed David. He threatened, if he did not hurry, find the wrench and bring it up to him, that he would come down and kick some sense into his empty, good for nothing head.

Terrified by his father's bitter words, David found the wrench, and hurrying to the packing box attempted to climb upon it. But David was a very small child, and the packing box was large, so that he found difficulty in mounting it. Then suddenly it happened. In his efforts to mount the box, he upset it. The ladder was unseated; and both the ladder and his father came hurtling to the ground. The plumber tried to break his fall by snatching at the rungs of the falling ladder, but without much success. In a matter of seconds it was all over. The falling father's feet struck his son's head. The plumber was badly shaken, little David was dead—the life kicked completely out of him by those very same feet with which but a moment before he had threatened the child.

The story of this accident swept swiftly through the village. Consequently, early that evening I went to call upon the stricken family. The plumber seemed almost to have been expecting me, for as soon as I knocked, he opened the door, saying, "Come in, preacher. It was a judgment of God upon me for my great wickedness."

I do not remember just what I said to that suffering man. I do not even remember what I said at the boy's funeral. However, it does not matter, for the Holy Spirit had interpreted little David's death to his father far better than any human speech could have done. The Spirit had shown the grief stricken man his sin in the tragedy it had produced. Nor had the plumber resisted the Spirit's light. Rather, he had humbly surrendered to it, repenting the evil that his life had been.

He said to me, "I did not mean to do it; but I did it; and if it had not been for my wicked temper it would never have happened. I had just threatened with an oath to come down and kick some sense into the child's head; and then I did come down and kicked the life quite out of it. Yes, preacher, it was a judgment of God on my wickedness. It was the natural consequence of just what my life had been."

Note now: the plumber did not have to accept this humiliating interpretation of the accident. He could have defended himself. He could have rationalized his son's death. He could have left buried in his own memory the recollection of the oaths and threats he had flung at the boy. This course, clearly lay wide open before him, and unquestionably his pride strongly urged him to adopt it.

The plumber, however, chose to accept the light of the Spirit's revelation, and to do so at the cost of his pride. He confessed his piled-up wickedness, and that it was his wickedness which was responsible for the accident that had killed his child. Shortly after David's death, he came to the Church, made public confession both of his sin and of his Saviour; and never again exploded into temper, or profaned the Saviour's sacred name.

I am aware that David's death came short of being a full analogy of Christ's cross in several respects.

Thus, David's death had just happened. The boy did not choose to die as Christ had done. The plumber, however, felt about the boy's death as if his vile temper had wrought it, and the child had actually accepted it. Christ had done just this, and the plumber seemed to see in David's sacrifice all the high values that belonged to Christ's. In any event David's death interpreted for the plumber his Saviour's Cross; and he found in it the same combination of searching judgment and wooing love that belonged to the latter.

There is something profound about this circumstance, and it reminds me of a much neglected text of St. Paul's. He speaks of filling up that which "is behind of the afflictions of Christ" (Colossians 1:24). He certainly does not mean that any human affliction can be added to Christ's, or that there could be any deficiency in His infinite sacrifice. He might, however, mean that our human afflictions can be assimilated to Christ's, as having a like value, and as helping us to understand that value.

Whether or not this would be a legitimate interpretation of the apostle's Colossian expression, I am convinced that it is true, and that all our human afflictions, accepted in humble adoring love, can be assimilated to Christ's cross, not indeed as enlarging it, but as belonging to it and interpreting it. In any event, this is what actually took place in the case of the plumber. Little David's death startled him, judged him, melted him, illumined him. He saw Christ's cross through it; and putting his humble trust in Him, he was transformed.

And so we come back now to the great text with which we started: "God loved the world in just this way, that he gave his only begotten Son, that whosoever believeth in him should not perish, but have everlasting life."

THE RESURRECTION

St. Matthew 28:6-7

"He is not here, for He is risen as He said. Come see the place where the Lord lay: and go quickly and tell His disciples that He is risen from the dead."

There are many historic tombs—Horatio Nelson's, Napoleon Bonaparte's, George Washington's; but in each instance those tombs are sacred because dust once animated by a creative spirit is preserved there. Only one tomb is open and empty, and significant because it is open and empty—the tomb of Jesus of Nazareth, which was long situated just outside the city of Jerusalem, and was later brought within that city by the extension of its north wall.

Jesus' tomb was, of course, one of the best known sights connected with the Holy City in the year 30. It was just west of the Genath Gate, near the great highway leading into the North. It was a cave in the side of a low hill, with its opening at the east end, facing the gate. In the year 40 Josephus tells us that a new wall was built definitely farther north, and the city was extended in that direction. In the year 70 the city was destroyed, and the walls, with the exception of a small section of the west wall, leveled. Such a destruction of the city, however, would not necessarily do any damage to a mere hole in the ground; and that it did not damage the Saviour's tomb is manifest from the circumstance that it was still intact when Emperor Hadrian rebuilt the city in the second century. At that

JESUS CHRIST IS LORD

time Hadrian ordered the Sepulchre desecrated to prevent worshippers from visiting it. He had it filled with refuse, and then buried beneath a mound of earth. Having built this up to a moderate height, he paved it over, and then erected upon it an altar to the goddess Venus. This pagan altar continued to desecrate and mark the spot until it was removed in the fourth century by order of Constantine. Constantine had decided to build over the sacred Tomb a great memorial to the Resurrection, and did so at his own expense, appointing Eusebius, bishop of Caesarea, his agent in effecting the work. We quote, now, from Eusebius' account of the great undertaking:

"Godless persons had thought entirely to remove from the eyes of men (the sacred tomb), supposing in their folly that they should be able effectually to obscure the truth. Accordingly they brought a quantity of earth from a distance . . . and covered the entire spot; then having raised this to a moderate height, they paved it with stone, concealing the holy cave beneath the massive mound. Then . . . they prepared on this foundation . . . a gloomy shrine . . . to the impure spirit they call Venus . . . offering detestable oblations on profane and accursed altars" (Life of Constantine, book III, chapter 25).

This desecrating structure Constantine ordered removed. Consequently, the pavement was torn up, the fill of refuse and dirt dug away, and the whole carted out of the city. Then "as soon as the original surface of the ground beneath the covering of earth appeared, immediately, and contrary to all expectation, the venerable and hallowed monument to our Saviour's Resurrection was discovered."

Eusebius does not mean to say that they were surprised at finding the Tomb, but merely that they were surprised at finding it uninjured either from its having been defaced, or from its having been buried for full two hundred years. The Tomb was intact; and so, when it had been cleansed, the great Church of the Resurrection was erected over it. This noble structure was four hundred and sixty-one feet long, and was in three sections; the rotunda of the Sepulchre, the court of Calvary, and the Helen chapel. Both the rotunda and the chapel were eighty-four feet high by one hundred and twenty-six feet wide.

Regrettably, Constantine cut away the hill of Calvary that the Tomb might stand out more boldly. The hill consequently is levelled, and the Tomb stands clear. The place where Jesus was crucified is marked in the south aisle of the court. It is some ninety feet from the Sepulchre; which agrees with St. John's description, that Joseph's new tomb was "in the same place where He was crucified" (St. John 10:41, 42).

The continuity of the records concerning this site is perfect. It was a definitely known location on Good Friday evening, when Joseph and Nicodemus entombed the body, while women of Jesus' company watched from the distance (St. Luke 23:55). It was even more definitely known at the end of the Sabbath, when its entrance was sealed by Rome, and a watch set upon it (St. Matt. 27:62ff). Easter morning, both the women and St. Peter and St. John visited it (St. John 20:1ff).

After that it was immediately a celebrated location, unquestionably visited by thousands. It was still being visited extensively a hundred years later, when Hadrian rebuilt Jerusalem in the second century, for he gave orders to desecrate it to make such visits impractical. Hadrian, however, only marked the sacred site by erecting his altar to Venus over it. Later, Constantine removed that pagan altar, and built the Church of the Resurrection in its place. That was at the beginning of the fourth century; and from that date forward this Church and its successors have continuously marked the cave and the couch where the supreme miracle of the centuries took place.

How greatly we wish that some of our scientists could have been there on Easter morning to observe and record the miracle as it took place. Our wish, however, is idle, for even if they had been there the miracle would have been too swift for them to have observed. You do not observe when matter is transformed into some new reality, as when an atom bomb is exploded. So when Jesus' mortal body was transformed into His body of glory the action was too swift for human observation. It took place, and His body burst forth from the Sepulchre, having definitely different powers from those which it had before. This is what we know from the testimony of the apostles, and this is all we could have known had a committee of our foremost scientists been present when the work was done.

"See," then, as the angels said to the women, "the place where the Lord lay." It is a cave, rectangular in form, with its entrance toward the east. The roof of the cave is low, about seven feet above the floor. The single stone couch within it lies to the right of the entrance. In front of the entrance, and to the left of it is a flat rock floor, about seven feet long and five feet deep. The single stone couch in the Tomb is slightly hollowed ,and stands above the floor just about twenty-four inches. There is ample room within the cave for a second couch. It seems probable that the left side was intended for such; but it has not been built. Since this was a new tomb, and the Son of God was both buried and raised there, it is easily understandable that Joseph of Arimathea chose never to finish it, but instead turned it over to the apostles as history's most sublime monument.

Joseph's tomb was not a pretentious structure; it was, however, the tomb of one of Jerusalem's most distinguished citizens; and the disciples were glad that their adored Master could be so appropriately buried. Here, on Easter morning, the resurrection miracle was wrought; and in Jesus' case the very substance of His body of death became also the substance of His body of glory. In our human resurrections, such an identity of substance is not necessary; but in Jesus' case it was necessary to register at the plane of history the certainty of His victory. The body of glory through which the risen Christ expressed Himself transcends our present sense powers: consequently the only way His victory could break into history was by the witness of the apostles to His appearances, and by the mysterious disappearance of His mortal body. Both of these wit-

JESUS CHRIST IS LORD 91

nesses are convincingly recorded in the Gospels.

Repeatedly in the New Testament you come upon the expression, "resurrection out from among the dead." It has a markedly different meaning from "resurrection of the dead." The second anticipates a universal experience, one fairly remote in the future. The first anticipates an individual experience that is always both victorious and near. St. Paul used this first expression to describe the goal toward which he continually both aspired and strove. He wanted to attain to the "out-resurrection, that out from among the dead" (Philippians 3:8). St. Peter used it also to describe the resurrection of Jesus on Easter morning; and with what vivid power it does describe that event. Jesus was literally lifted out from among the dead, clothed for Eternal life.

Death is, of course, a very difficult idea as applied to men and women. Death is incongruous with man's aspiring moral personality. One who bears the image of God; who thinks with the Divine reason; who feels the same moral obligation which God recognizes as F holiness; who even attains to worship Him—clearly such a one should not die. We, however, are so accustomed to the naturalistic interpretation of death that we are almost unconscious of the violence it does to our aspiring natures. But death does not belong to aspiring moral man. It belongs only to disfigured man —to man who has lost his moral and aspiring way. Had man not lost his way, had he not given himself to proud self-centered motives, God's very moral glory would have compelled Him to have lifted such a creature clear of natural death. But man did sin. Man did make choice of the proud self-centered motive; and as a consequence he has filled history with tragedy. What might have happened if man had not sinned is manifestly mere speculation. The evident fact of history is that man sinned, and that God either thrust him back within, or left him within the severe limitations of the natural order.

Nevertheless death is incongruous to aspiring moral man; and the age-long anguish with which he has experienced it bears witness to this incongruity. Death is doubtless fit enough to sinful man; but to perfect man —a man who never appeared save once in the whole sweep of history—it manifestly is not fit. Consequently when the sinless man appeared and died, God had to do something about it. This was God's moral necessity, even as it is a necessity of man's moral reason to appreciate God's necessity.

We dare not tolerate any hesitation at this point. Moral necessity is just as real a principle as rational necessity. Experience discovers four certainties—rational necessity, moral necessity, aesthetic necessity, and what Professor Brightman used to call "bruit facts." Philosophy is grounded in the first, religion in the second and third, science in the fourth; but all four of these necessities are characteristic points of view with which the human consciousness confronts experience; and their united operation concludes one truth. This is the mind of man; and if he does violence to this mind, or uses it in an incomplete and fragmentary way, he must not be surprised when he arrives at vanity.

The fact is truth is necessarily approached by a three lane highway; and all three lanes must be simultaneously in operation, or truth will fail. Materialism, Naturalism, Behaviorism, Communism are speculations of men who traveled one, or at most two lanes, neglecting the others. All these speculations deny man's freedom, the authority of his moral sense, the significance of his impress of the infinite; and because they do, they unfound his intellectual powers. Necessarily they make truth impossible. The fact is they even make science impossible. The academic freedom with which the universities are so greatly concerned becomes rather humorous when it insists on the right of a professor to teach the impossibility of human freedom. Evidently, if there is no such value as human freedom, academic freedom cannot be a possibility!

But Materialism, Naturalism, etc., are just irrational speculations. The transcendent is necessary not only to religion but to thought. Without its recognition religion, truth, and life all three necessarily fail. When we exclude the transcendent, there can be nothing remaining but process; and if all is process, truth is fate. Reality becomes thus an immense meaningless kaleidoscope, without even the advantage of a transcendent seeing eye. The recognition of the transcendent is thus fundamental at once to thought, to life and to religion; and he who denies it, whether he labels himself a Materialist, a Naturalist, or a Communist, will find it necessary both to think and live outside the bounds by which he has arbitrarily limited reality.

But once we have admitted the reality of the transcendent, the evidences of Jesus' Easter morning victory over human death become little short of a demonstration.

In the first place the empty sepulchre is completely undeniable. It is certified by an imperial act of desecration which both buried and marked the site of the Saviour's Tomb until the Church was sufficiently established to take over the sacred cave and preserve it for the ages.

In the second place, the risen manifestations of Jesus are to say the least, challenging. All but two were experienced by groups of men, not by individuals: and those experiences were a formulated statement within ten years of the actual event. St. Paul almost certainly received them from St. Peter; and the most probable date for this communication is when he spent two weeks with the Chief Apostle before retiring to Tarsus (Galatians 1:18). St. Paul grounded his Gospel upon this formulation when he began to preach in Corinth, and reduced it to writing soon afterward (First Corinthians 15:3-8).

In the third place, this glorious witness to the resurrection fact both corresponds to and fulfills the universal aspirations of the human soul. Nor can it be called "wishful thinking" when one affirms the truth of those values toward which all men everywhere aspire. Edgar Brightman's "bruit facts" are no more commandingly certain than the universal outreachings of the human soul.

This, then is the glorious witness with which the

Church annually energizes faith. It helps men to believe large, instead of to believe small—to believe in the sublime and aspiring, instead of in the degrading and the frustrating. And these are the two outlooks upon reality between which men must choose. There is no third possibility. Starting with the affirmation of God, the whole of the large faith becomes sure. Starting without God, every sublimity must be surrendered. Righteousness, truth, freedom, all must be surrendered. Even science has to be reduced to a meaningless positivism.

We confront, then, the choice we are making—have to make, as we face reality. Many years ago I read a very great book by James Orr, entitled, *The Christian View of God and the World*. One of the arguments of that book was that truth continually divides up and down. Every school of thought will become two. One of these schools will react toward larger ideas and Christ, while the other will descend more deeply into despair and pessimism. Of course Professor Orr's generalization is true. It even has to be true: for every intermediate position between large faith and complete despair is untenable. All Matrialists, Naturalists, Behaviorists, Communists, when they attain to full intellectual grasp, will be pessimists. And every man who reacts from pessimism, when he attains to full intellectual grasp, will believe in God and Christ and righteousness and truth and destiny These are the two possibilities of truth. Between is nothing but incomplete thinking and illusion.

THE MEANING OF THE ASCENSION

St. Luke 24:50-51

"And He led them out as far as Bethany, and He lifted up His hands and blessed them. And it came to pass while He blessed them, He was parted from them, and carried up into heaven."

St. John 16:7

"It is expedient for you that I go away, for if I go not away the Comforter will not come unto you; but if I depart I will send Him unto you."

St. John 20:17

"Touch me not, for I am not yet ascended unto my Father, but . . . I ascend."

St. Matthew 28:18

"All authority is given unto me in heaven and in earth . . . and lo I am with you always, even unto the end of the world."

First Corinthians 15:25-26

"For He must reign until He hath put all enemies under His feet; and the last enemy that shall be destroyed is death."

Jesus was certainly crucified on a Preparation of the Sabbath which was also a Preparation of the Passover. The *Jewish Mishna* unites with the *Fourth Gospel* in so designating the particular Friday when Jesus was crucified (St. John 13:1).

Jesus' sepulchre was just as certainly found open and empty on Easter morning: for the Gospels all affirm it, and the Jewish authorities, admitting the

JESUS CHRIST IS LORD

fact, explain it by the absurd libel that the disciples stole the body.

Everything is remarkably definite about this wonderful Christian record. The grave clothes in the Tomb were carefully described—the napkin was in a place by itself, separate from the rest of the bandages. Jesus' appearances, too, were both definite and illusive. He appeared and disappeared. They saw Him and recognized Him; and yet while they were communing with Him He disappeared from before their eyes. He appeared, also in different forms, and sometimes they were slow to recognize Him, experiencing something of surprise, wanting to, and yet fearing to ask questions (Luke 24:16, John 21:12).

Jesus' last manifestation before the Ascension was to a considerable group of His followers. There were a hundred and twenty of them. He walked with them up the slope of the Mount of Olives, and to the neighborhood of Bethany. Olivet is one of the highest mountains in Palestine. It tops Mount Zion, overlooking Jerusalem; and from this vantage point practically every scene of Jesus' life lay, as it were, clustered about His feet. Bethlehem, where He was born, was to the west, a little south of Jerusalem. Nazareth, where He grew to manhood, was in the north, a low hill on the edge of the valley of Esdraelon, definitely east of Carmel. The Lake of Galilee with its little ring of cities, where so much of His public ministry had been enacted, lay up the Jordan valley. Farther north was the snow capped peak of Hermon, on which He had been transfigured. Golgotha and its mysterious empty sepulchre were almost at His feet. They were hidden from sight by the western walls of Jerusalem.

All these places and events lay there in panorama before Him; and Jesus may have reviewed the tremendous story of His life immediately before He recommissioned His followers saying: "Ye shall be witnesses unto me in Jerusalem, and in all Judea, and in Samaria, and unto the uttermost parts of the earth" (Acts 1:8). Then, standing there in the midst of history, and in the midst of His disciples, He raised His hands in blessing. His act was probably symbolical, and may have referred to His promised commanding of the Holy Spirit upon them. His hands would be a proper symbol of His sovereign authority, just as His breath was a proper symbol of His living spirit-consciousness. In the Upper Room, at His first appearance to the Twelve after His resurrection, He had blown His breath upon them, saying, "Receive ye the Holy Spirit." Of course His reference had been to His promised gift of the Spirit, which would follow immediately His enthronement in the Infinite.

Then, even as He was speaking to them, He began to ascend. They watched Him rise. They saw Him disappear into a cloud. Evidently He had now returned to the Infinite. He had been restored to the glory which He had had with the Father before the worlds (St. John 17:5). Already He had announced His sovereignty—"All authority is given unto me both in heaven and on earth" (St. Matthew 28:18). They thought of Him as established upon an invisible throne,

JESUS CHRIST IS LORD

reigning both within history and above it; and He would continue thus to reign until He had subdued every enmity, completely overcome world-evil, and brought to an end the tragic blight of human death. Then, at last after all these things had been accomplished, He would return visibly, out of the Infinite; and men would gaze upon His returning even as they had gazed upon His going. In this climatic event the universe would become what God had meant it to be from the beginning; and in this perfect universe God would be perfectly expressed.

Such are the facts of the Ascension; but the event is very much more than an interesting fact. It has deep meaning. Jesus was conscious that His going away was important. He had said to the Twelve, "It is expedient for you that I go away" (St. John 16:7).

Jesus had meant two things by this statement. First, He had meant that His disappearing out of history would be earth's poor record of a great heavenly event—the Son's re-establishment in the glory of the Father. Second, He had meant that the disappearance of His vivid flesh would give men a better chance to appreciate Him as inwardly and immediately revealed within their deepest consciousness.

Both of these meanings are superlatively important. The Spirit cannot begin His revealing work until Christ has been glorified; and since this work is necessary also to man's salvation, this also must wait upon the glorification of Jesus.

This is a most important truth. We are attempting to understand something internal to the life of

God, and because we are, we must think both humbly and searchingly. It was perfectly clear to Jesus that He had to be glorified both before the Spirit could be given, and before human salvation could have its effective beginning. As I understand Jesus, He saw that He had to be taken back into the Infinite, carrying His earth history with Him, before it would be possible for God to command the Holy Spirit to abide upon believing, but none the less, sinful men.

We must never forget that God's love is moral love, and that because God's love has this moral quality, He cannot easily live in intimate relations with sinful men. As repentant and believing sinners, men have indeed denied both their sins and themselves; but they are none the less sin blemished both in their habits, their impulses, and their thoughts. It will be the Spirit's residence within them that will change these bitter blemishes. But the Spirit will not accomplish this in a moment, and so God's glory must be fully defended before the Spirit's intimate identification with sinners can begin.

God could not be satisfied to judge men without also expressing His love. Consequently He accepted the Cross.

God could not be satisfied just to express His love without also initiating a great program of salvation. Consequently He gave the Holy Spirit to abide.

But God could not be satisfied to love sinners and to live intimately with them unless His moral glory was fully defended against every possibility of misexpression and of misunderstanding. Consequently

Easter and Ascension had to follow Good Friday, and the whole great redemptive sacrifice had to be fully completed before the Spirit could be given to abide.

I am deeply sensitive to the costliness for God of the Spirit's intimate residence within the consciousness of repentant, believing, forgiven sinners. We men and women come very slowly into sainthood. The New Birth is of course an instantaneous work, but the transforming consequences of the New Birth upon the believer's habits and viewpoints is a long process. Yet during all this time the Holy Spirit must dwell intimately with sinful men. He must share all their darkened understandings, all their crude behaviors. The holy God can and does endure this; but He is able to endure it only because His holiness is continually defended by that immense self-expression He has fixed forever in His glory by the return of the Crucified Christ.

This is the primary meaning of the Ascension. Jesus with His acquired history returns into the Infinite. He is enthroned there. But the Ascension has also a secondary meaning. Man's knowledge of God—of Christ—is twofold. It is inward, and it is also outward. It is an immediate experience of Presence and it is also an outward revelation of an objective person. The first of these experiences is delicate, like the loveliness of the moonlight. The second is dominating, like the blazing glory of the sun. And just as it is difficult to experience the moon while the sun is shining, so it is difficult to experience Christ as inward Presence while His outward form is flooding one's senses.

It was the importance of becoming established in this inward experience of Presence which Jesus had in mind when He forbade Mary Magdalene to grasp Him by the feet (St. John 20:17). Christians need to be deeply established in their inward knowledge of Christ, before they begin to live in contact with the thrilling splendor of His outward revelation. St. Paul's experience of Christ's outward manifestation on the Damascus road passed quickly. It was succeeded by the Spirit's revelation of Christ's inward Presence. The outward manifestation was only restored much later at the end of St. Paul's probationary career.

Salvation is thus continually an immense interaction between God and man, and between inward and outward experiences. The Divine side of this interaction is, of course, the greater. No man can save himself. Indeed, the mood of arrogant self-sufficiency comes very near to being the central motive of all sin's falsehoods. Jesus definitely recognized this mood as sinful. He said, "The Son can do nothing of himself" (St. John 5:19). He felt it necessary for Him continually to be reaching into the life of His Father; and it is only as men attain to a similar attitude of free dependence upon Him that the universe can be completed, or men's individual lives become blessed.

But to return to the Ascension—there is always an inward as well as an outward truth. The first is silent, creative, the second is dramatic, commanding. Thus God is eternal truth, while creation is truth's dramatic expression. Similarly, God's moral suffer-

ing because of human sin is as old and as long as sin; but only in time and in the Cross did God achieve its dramatic expression. Once more, the restoration of Christ to the eternal glory is a great inner truth; and the Ascension is its dramatic expression.
They are important to men. They are important to God. God is putting every motive and movement of His Eternal Life into expression in His cosmic poem; and it is only as we appreciate the universe and history from this point of view that we have seen it as God thinks of it, and values it.

Consequently, both Creation and Redemption are Divine interests more profoundly than they are human interests; and they are outward values as definitely as they are inward values. God expressed is a richer value than God unexpressed. Therefore, whenever a sublime spiritual truth is put into dramatic outward expression, something of immense significance has been accomplished. So we have the Cross, the Resurrection, the Ascension, Judgment Day, and the second coming of Christ.

Angels announced the Second Coming in the very midst of the Ascension. It would be the next great dramatic event in cosmic history. It would be the climactic dramatization of Christ's eternal kingship. It would be an event at once natural, and yet also transcendent. Nor will the clear Christian thinker need to feel any timidity toward the transcendent, for men can neither live nor think without making use of it So on Ascension Day, while the apostles were standing gazing into the skies, they became aware that angels were addressing them. They said, "Ye men of Galilee, why stand ye gazing into the heavens? This same Jesus which is taken from you into heaven, shall so come again in like manner as ye have seen him go away into heaven" (Acts 1:10, 11).

This announcement was the final word in the first chapter of earth's supreme story—"The beginning of the Gospel of Jesus Christ the Son of God." The second chapter is all about us in the fact of the universal Church, and in the fact of our greatly modified and liberated human society. The third chapter is now trembling upon the very threshold of events. The call of the hour is to maintain an attitude of alert, believing expectancy: for "in such an hour as ye think not the Son of man cometh" (St. Matthew 24:44).

THE GIFT OF THE HOLY SPIRIT TO ABIDE
St. John 16:7

"Nevertheless I tell you the truth; It is expedient for you that I go away; for if I go not away the Comforter will not come unto you; but if I depart I will send Him unto you."

There is no teaching of the New Testament more clearly stated than that of the reality and necessity for some sort of spiritual new birth. The natural man, with his natural viewpoint and motives cannot attain to his destiny. We are called to the knowledge of God, and in that knowledge to live lives of all-embracing reverence; but the driving intensity of our dominating self-consciousness discovers God to be both pale and remote, while our fellow beings are not only remote, but comparatively speaking, unimportant. Self is the one commanding value. We divide reality into two halves, as William James used to say—ourselves, and all the rest, God, men, things.

This is the imprisoning consciousness by which nature shuts the natural man away from fulfillment and destiny. He can, indeed, conceive ideas which tower above it, but he cannot energize them into life. He can approve that which is good, but he cannot perform it. He lacks the effective motive to good. His dominating self-consciousness makes him inevitably a lord, and only his conscience tells him that he ought to be a brother. The difference between the glad selfless devotion of a mother, and the meticulously correct services of a trained nurse kept upon her work overtime, might suggest the inadequacy of the natural man's point of view.

The natural man is thus necessarily incomplete. He is driven by his dominating sense of self and his thirst of the infinite. He is a solitary, lonely, burning sense of "I", who does not know any way of coming into intimate contact with *other*. He is a lost personality—lost in the infinite desert of himself.

Confronting this experience, even in the innermost circle of the men who surround Him and yet quarreled over *chief seats*, Jesus said to them, "It is expedient for you that I go away." He meant it was important for them to lose Him outwardly, in order that they might possess Him inwardly, for only the Infinite Other, Spirit revealed, can come close enough to man's dominating self to replace his natural ego-drive with a sense of rich, overflowing fellowship.

To experience this ego-drive of the natural self-consciousness replaced by the overflowing fellowship of the Spirit's revelation of Christ is salvation. Because this new experience is one of infinite abundance, it satisfies what had been man's infinite thirst. Because it makes man consciously at home in the Infinite, it gives him a sense of possessing the truth. He possesses the truth in its ultimate meaning even while he is pursuing its details. Because it is shot full of moral concern, it is majestic like the glory of God. This is the rapture of the Spirit energized experience, which replaces the dissatisfied loneliness of man's solitary "I" with the rich, abounding fellowship of his new sense—"Christ and I."

Strikingly enough men seem to shrink from this experience. Indeed, they even seem to flee from it, preferring to stand alone, independent. So the exponent of naturalistic philosophy chooses to degrade himself to a dying animal for no other reason than that he may experience the superficial thrill of feeling himself intellectually self-sufficient. He would rather be a self-sufficient dying animal, than a dependent son of God. Communism is one of the absurd expedients turned to by men who have repudiated God for the brief satisfaction of feeling self-sufficient. Discovering the inevitable littleness of the God-denying life, they have tried to recover some sense of meaning and inclusiveness in an all-embracing materialism. They seem quite to miss the circumstance that the only inclusiveness provided by Communism is that of an all-embracing degradation. All men are equally dying animals, confronting an all-engulfing darkness, that can experience neither hope nor truth.

I vividly remember the night when I first knew the sheer wonder of the experience of the Infinite Presence. It was expansive. It was abounding. It was tenderly intimate. It created a new expression to describe itself. I found myself using the words, *my God consciousness*. I analyzed what had happened to me by the standard of ideas I had just learned in philosophy. I had learned that personality manifested itself in five powers of the mind—consciousness, emotion, conscience, will, and self-awareness. I asked myself in which of these areas my new experience had taken place. I saw instantly it was not in any of the first four. With respect to these nothing had happened. In the fifth area, however, there had been an important change. My self-awareness was definitely different. Before it had been a burning lonely sense of "I". Now it had become an abounding sense of "We"—the Infinite and I, Christ and I.

This experience took place at the threshold of the holiday season in 1902. It was just before I went home for Christmas. At home that Christmas I was invited to preach, and my sermon was an analysis of my new experience grounded upon the text, "If any man is in Christ, he is a new creation" (II Cor. 5:17).

St. Paul calls this Spirit revelation of the Infinite Other, "the earnest of the Spirit"—God's down payment on His promise of Eternal Life; and it is indeed literally such, for this intimate revelation of God is that knowledge of the true God and Jesus Christ, which Jesus said was Eternal Life.

Any experience as great as this new revelation of the Infinite Other necessarily has immense consequences. I found it changed the whole organization of my life. Life had been a thing of struggling effort. It became a thing of abounding power. I no longer tried to do right; I just lived out the motives that seemed to flood up within me. God had become intimately real. He was no longer One whom I proved by formal arguments, but One whom I knew as a living presence, a necessary reality. I knew Him as I knew right and wrong, as I knew that space had three dimensions. The experience of the Spirit's revelation was like the gift of a new insight. In nature I knew reason, beauty, duty. In the Spirit I now knew God. He was just as necessary, just as unescapable as the laws of reason, aesthetics, and morals.

Manifestly God must always have intended man to live at this higher plane of awareness. His presence is necessary to the completing of man's personality. Man without the revelation of God might be compared to plant life without the shining of the sun. Plants were made to be energized by the shining of the sun, and men were made to be illumined by the revelation of God. Jesus said, "I live because of the Father" (John 6:57), meaning that the fellowship of the Father gave constant enrichment and direction to His living; or again, "The Son can do nothing of himself" (John 5:19). He speaks what He hears with the Father, and does what He sees (John 5:20-30).

The law of life both for the Eternal Son, and for created sons, is that of glad, humble, dependence. Man was not intended to be complete in himself, but rather to be complete in an uninterrupted relation to God. It is the Covenant of Abraham—"Walk in my presence" (Genesis 17:1). When man is without this completing sense of Presence, he is inevitably lonely. Joseph Fort Newton used to say, that men are almost universally lonely—lonely and afraid; and of course they are. The burning experience of self-consciousness is inevitably lonely; and since self-driven man cannot fulfill the demands of the moral ought, men are also inevitably guilty and afraid.

All down man's centuries he has been in flight from God. There are two chief reasons for this flight.

First, man's pride makes him want to be self-sufficient. Second, man's sense of failure makes him want to get away from God's immense moral demand. We get a vivid expression of man's flight from God in the practices of the Negrillos of Africa. They believe in a supreme God whom they call the great He. They have, however, very little to do with this God. Their every day religion is concerned with demons, ghosts, goblins; and they only address the great He in time of tribal danger or calamity. Apart from such circumstances, if the great He should seem to become manifest at any time, the Negrillos would instantly flee. Thus, they have a superstition that when their camp fires loudly crack in burning, it is a sign that the great He has found their encampment; and their instant reaction is fear and flight.

God, as we have said, never intended man to live thus lonely and afraid; and it is the glory of Jesus that He never did. His experience of personality was always the sense of self enriched by the sense of Presence. He exclaimed one day to His disciples, "Behold the hour cometh, yea, is now come, that ye shall be scattered every man to his own, and shall leave me alone." And then interrupting His announcement, He instantly added, "And yet I am not alone, because the Father is with me" (John 16:32).

This uninterrupted sense of Presence was both the power and the glory of Jesus' life. He felt infinitely close to His Father. It seemed that no one else knew Him (Matt. 11:27). The one all-including tragedy of the world was that it did not know God. He exclaimed

JESUS CHRIST IS LORD 111

one day in prayer, "O righteous Father, the world hath not known thee!" and then added the contrast truth, "But I have known thee" (John 17:25). Because Jesus was enriched with this experience life was continually transfigured for Him. His Father clothed the lilies of the field with a radiance surpassing the glory of Solomon, knew each tiny sparrow both in its flight and in its fall, commanded His sun to shine upon the evil and the good, and sent His rain upon the just and upon the unjust (St. Luke 12:27f, also 6, and St. Matt. 5:45).

Jesus' life was thus literally a God saturated life; and this peculiarity glorified even the tragedy of His cross. Hanging there in agony, He still knew a transfiguring exaltation. In comparison with the sadist crowd which was mocking His agony He felt strangely enriched, so that He pitied their impoverishment. Here, indeed, is a real measure of the power of Jesus' sense of Presence. It lifted Him so effectively above His pain, that He felt a great pity for those who were mocking Him, and prayed, "Father, forgive them" they are damning themselves, and think they are me (compare Luke 23:34).

This enriched consciousness is man as God meant him to be; but man's pride of self-sufficiency caused him to choose to stand alone, independent. And so seeking to enlarge himself, he has ensmalled himself; seeking to exalt himself, he has degraded himself: and this proud choice has been peculiarly the blight of the twentieth century, which at its beginning thought progress secure, and man so good that he only needed a little cultural guidance. What a terrific change has taken place in the years since the close of the first World War. Now we know that progress can only be won by toil and sacrifice, and that far from being naturally good, man, yes, educated man, is capable of all the barbarities of Nero, Attila, and Genghis Khan.

Let me clothe this New Testament experience of an enriched self-consciousness — a *fellowship consciousness*, with a unique experience I read some years ago. It was in a modern biography, the title of which I have forgotten. But on a certain day, one of the common run of secularized personalities we frequently meet, got out of bed with a feeling of depression. He was discouraged. He was dissatisfied. He was lonely. He was afraid. In this state of mind he went down town to his work. In the course of the morning, his mood grew darker. Doubtless some aggravating circumstances had occasioned his mood in the first place, and some added experience of the same kind had now deepened it. He felt literally sick, and so in the middle of the morning said to his boss, "Something's wrong with me. I guess I'll have to go home."

Shortly before noon his wife heard someone letting himself in at the front door, and stepping into the hall, saw her husband. Completely surprised, she exclaimed, "Why, Jim, is something wrong?"

"No," he answered, "I just feel down, so I'm going back to bed."

So saying, he went dejectedly upstairs, and did just that. In a few minutes his wife followed him into their bedroom, and sitting down upon the counter-

JESUS CHRIST IS LORD 113

pane, began drumming a tune upon it.

"What am I drumming?" she asked engagingly.

"Haven't an idea," was his indifferent reply.

"Three guesses," she replied still invitingly.

Uninterested, but just to cooperate, he answered, "Tipperary."

"Wrong!" she exclaimed. "Guess again."

"Yankee Doodle," he guessed.

"Wrong again!" she told him. "Guess once more."

"It's a long, long trail a-winding," he said.

"Still wrong. You could never guess. I was drumming, 'Rock of Ages.' You say the words as I drum it, and you'll see."

She drummed again, and he said the words in his mind:

"Rock of ages, cleft for me,
Let me hide myself in Thee.
Let the water and the blood
From thy riven side which flowed
Be of sin the double cure,
Save from wrath and make me pure."

At first he only said the words; and then almost unconsciously he began to pray them. He was really reaching outside his frustrated life into the life of God. And suddenly, silently, there was a response. The Spirit revealed an infinitely tender and enriching Presence.

"Something has happened!" exclaimed the lonely man. "As you were drumming 'Rock of Ages,' I prayed it: and as I prayed, something wonderful happened. It seemed that a new Presence took possession of me. It was a something plus that came exceedingly near me, and that seemed at once to comfort and strengthen me."

Immediately this sick man got out of bed. He was sick no longer. In the early afternoon he was back at his place of business.

Such narratives of swift deliverance could be multiplied literally thousands of times. They have been occurring now for near two thousand years, and always the experience has been at once the same and different. The Spirit has revealed Christ as an intimate presence, and His presence has instantly changed man's self-consciousness from one of lonely, dissatisfied longing into fellowship and overflowing abundance.

There is a remarkable succession of these Spirit enriched personalities who have appeared down the centuries — St. Paul, St. Augustine, Luther, Wesley. Survey quickly this experience of Presence as it came to each of them.

St. Paul's experience of the Spirit was by no means that outward vision of Jesus which was given to him on the Damascus Road. This experience did doubtless involve some form of inward empowering, for while St. Paul's fellow travelers realized something extraordinary was going on, they did not see the heavenly figure, whom St. Paul saw in blinding glory (Acts 26:14). This experience itself, however, was outward, and therefore lacking in that mysterious intimacy characteristic of all inward revelations of the Infinite.

As outward, this experience could and did challenge St. Paul's will; but it could not, and did not transform his basic self-consciousness. This greater work was yet to be done. God left him for three days just to sit in the dark—to remember—to think, and then he sent Ananias to him, and the Holy Spirit was given (Acts 9:9).

This second experience St. Paul describes as God's "revealing of his Son in me" (Galatians 1:15, 16); and he speaks also of the enduring consciousness which it produced, as "Christ living in me" (Galatians 2:20). It seemed literally to the apostle, that while he still lived beyond the Spirit's revelation of Christ, it was less he, himself, who was living, than it was Christ. Christ's presence seemed to pervade him, and this mystical experience became the central reality of his gospel.

St. Augustine's conversion was different, and yet similar. He too had been long engaged in a religious struggle. His struggle also came to a climax in an outward revelation which was audible, and then an inward revelation which was life transforming. The outward experience Augustine describes as a voice commanding him to pick up the scroll of *Romans* and read. "Take and read" were the words he heard. Immediately picking up the scroll his eyes fell upon words at the end of the 13th chapter—"Put ye on the Lord Jesus Christ, and make no provision for the flesh to fulfill the lusts thereof" (Romans 13:14). The soul of Augustine responded obediently to the call, which, now, had become inward as well as outward;

and as he responded the intimate work was done, Christ became the enriching master of his life.

In Martin Luther's case the revelation of Christ came as he was climbing the Santa Scala upon his naked knees. A word from the Scriptures seemed to appear within his consciousness with living power. Charles G. Finney describes a similar experience which came to him as he prayed in the woods. The particular words that burst into Martin Luther's mind as he climbed the stairs that day were, "The just shall live by faith." The effect was electric. Luther rose upon his feet, a thing which was never done, and turning walked down the stairs. Several scholars have called this story in question, but the distinguished Professor Jacobs, late of Mt. Airy Seminary, quotes the Reformer's son as certifying it.

Precisely what did happen to Luther? The answer of course, is the Spirit challenged the outwardness of Luther's habitual formalism with the inwardness of the Gospel. Luther had been made to see that salvation arose in the believer's reach outside himself that fixes all his hope in Christ. With what power this new intimate experience speaks in the Reformer's later writings. Take a single illustration—his reformation hymn:

> "Did we in our strength confide,
> Our striving would be losing;
> Were not the right man on our side,
> The man of God's own choosing;
> Dost ask whom that may be,
> Christ Jesus it is He:

JESUS CHRIST IS LORD 117

Lord Sabbaoth is His name,
From age to age the same,
And He must win the battle."

The fourth name in the creative succession is John Wesley, and he too had difficulty in getting free from the viewpoint and motive of self-sufficiency. Being so deeply committed to self, he found trust outside himself exceedingly difficult.

There is nothing astonishing about this. Strong men, and especially proud men find more difficulty in repudiating self than in any other sacrifice. The coarse sinner is already without reputation, but the gentleman, the moral man, the pharisee is somebody, and finds it hard to deny himself.

Wesley of course had long realized that God would have to judge him with mercy; but it was self, nevertheless, whom God would judge; and so his hope of salvation depended upon his making that self as nearly respectable as possible. Wesley, consequently, notwithstanding his consecration, had remained a deeply self-centered personality.

At last however, he came to see himself as lost and hopeless: and when the soloist at St. Paul's sang at Evening Prayer, "Out of the depths have I cried unto Thee," Wesley felt she was singing his experience. Later that day he went to a meeting of a few laymen in a room in Aldersgate Street, and there while the leader was reading from Luther's introduction to one of his commentaries on an epistle by St. Paul, Wesley moved his confidence from self to Christ. He began to trust Christ wholly, and immediately Christ was revealed as an intimate presence within him. The natural consequence of this tender revelation was the strange warming of his heart; but that blessed emotion was only a result of his experience; it was not the experience itself. Wesley expressed a clearer apprehension of what had actually taken place within him when he wrote of his waking moment the next day, that the first name in his mind and on his lips was, "Jesus, Master."

The Spirit's intimate revelation of Christ is thus the innermost reality of every Christian experience, no matter what may be its outward form or attending circumstances. The lonely, dissatisfied "I" of nature is enriched by an intimate revelation of the Infinite. The sense of loneliness is replaced by the sense of fellowship, the sense of dissatisfaction is replaced by the sense of a blessed fullness that overflows. The sense of "Christ and I," glad, satisfied, overflowing has replaced the dissatisfied, aspiring, pursuing sense of lonely "I".

I ought to pause long enough to protect the reader against one possible misunderstanding. The Spirit's revelation of Presence is not immediately a fully mature Christian experience. When the believer dies unto his former pride, and reaches outside himself to lay hold upon the grace of God in Christ, both his self-denial and his faith are limited by his own very inadequate understandings. After he has walked in the fellowship of the Presence for a time, his understandings will be greatly enlarged. His repentance can then be made very much fuller; his trust in Christ can be made very much larger. If the believer takes advantage of this enlarged possibility, making a very much more complete self-denial, and a very much more complete venture of trust, the Spirit's revelation of Presence will become a very much richer experience. He will see all his ideas and purposes as Christ also sees them, and the love of Christ will enrich and command his every self-conscious moment. This is Perfect Love as Olin Alfred Curtis describes the experience. It is not absolute perfection, but a state of perfection sufficiently mature to make love the commanding motive in every self-conscious moment of life. Sub-personal actions may still come short of being Christian; but all such sub-personal actions will be immediately repudiated the instant the Christian rises into full fellowship-consciousness (his self-consciousness as enriched by the revelation of Presence).

In Wesley's case this deeper experience came to him out of a crisis involving his health. His life work had begun, and was going forward powerfully; and then his health failed. He became subject to hemorrhages, his physical prospect became most discouraging. Here was a real test of his will to trust Christ regardless, and Wesley took full advantage of the opportunity. He went on with his work as he was able, awaiting with confidence the full manifestation of the Divine will. The result was the Spirit revealed Christ with an intimate fullness that caused him to write in his journal that he was able to see every idea and every emotion just as it arose in his heart, and whether it was right before God or no.

Such an intimate and powerful sense of Presence is indeed a commanding experience. It might be compared to locking arms with the Saviour as one makes his journey down the trail of life; and such a powerful sense of Presence is necessarily life-commanding. There is no room in such a life for jealousies, greed, fear, hatred, contempt, covetousness. There is of course room in such a Christ enriched life for subpersonal actions, and even for hasty and unwise actions, but there is no room for a Christ unconscious personal choice.

There are three other characteristic values in the experience of the Spirit's coming to abide which it is important to discriminate.

The first is that the Spirit's revelation of Presence gives one a sense of possessing Truth. Jesus even called Him, "The Spirit of Truth" because His coming would do this characteristic work. The word *Truth* here must not be understood as embracing *all facts;* but it can be understood as embracing *all meaning*. Jesus, as incarnate, having for a period laid aside His glory did not know the mystery of the atom as Robert Millikan did; but He did know the unity of His life with the Father, and this is the really important value in truth. Beyond the Resurrection His eternal glory was restored; involving all knowledge and all power, but His grasp of the meaning of life had never been interrupted.

The second of these important values is that the coming of the Spirit produces a number of practical attitudes that Jesus and the apostles called fruits.

JESUS CHRIST IS LORD

These practical attitudes have very great value for living. St. Paul gives a partial list of them—love, joy, peace, steadfastness, gentleness, goodness, faith (Galatians 5:22). These fruits do not of course condition or produce salvation; they, rather, manifest it. We are not saved because these fruits are developed in our lives. We are saved because Christ is revealed within our consciousness, and these fruits manifest the reality of His creative presence.

Finally, the revelation of Presence is the actual beginning of Eternal Life; for Eternal Life is precisely the intimate, immediate knowledge of the Infinite. All down history men have been seeking fulfillment where no such experience can be found—in pride, in power, in multiplication of things. Communism is now undertaking to do this by a program of coercion and collectivization. It is also attempting to seal the one door by which the human race can attain to fulfillment—the knowledge of God. It classifies the very idea of God as a deadening opiate which puts to sleep man's resentment, and so enables some upper class to enslave him. "Religion is the opiate of the people," it proclaims.

How tragically perverse! How proudly false this bitter idea! Communism itself has nothing to offer men but slavery—the most extreme slavery human arrogance ever has conceived; and its promises of good are mere empty words—words that can appear to have content to none save the unthinking. No mere accumulation of things can ever satisfy infinitely aspiring man. No equality between himself and other men, but at the plane of dying animals, can fulfill his majestic self-consciousness. Man is completely hopeless at the plane of nature. Either he must attain to the transcendent or surrender to pessimism. An impress of the infinite is upon man, and either he must attain to the knowledge of God, or his life becomes an unfulfilled contradiction.

> Now make me one with Christ,
> Disclose His presence near;
> Come, Holy Ghost, His whispered truth
> I thirst, I pant to hear.
> Reveal Him near as wind
> That wets my cheek with rain;
> Reveal Him near as me, myself,
> As near me as my pain.
> Reveal the Heavenly Christ,
> Who once for sin didst die;
> His mystic Presence will enlarge
> My cramping 'prisoning "I".
> 'Twas so I prayed, and then,
> At once the work was done—
> Christ's Presence, Fellowship, enriched
> A *self* into a *son*.
> I'm still myself, but more—
> Myself and Him made one
> No more I seek my wilful way,
> But shout when His is done.
> To all I now belong,
> As all are mine, I see;
> Christ's holy love embracing all
> Relates them all to me.

Great rapture thrills my mind,
God's glory all is given;
Christ's Presence makes life overflow;
He changes earth to heaven.

THE OUT—RESURRECTION—
THAT OUT FROM AMONG THE DEAD

Philippians 3:11

"That I might attain to the out-resurrection, that out from among the dead."

When St. Paul speaks of the supreme goal of his life as being, *to attain to the out-resurrection, that out from among the dead,* he is manifestly not thinking of the general resurrection. Professor Vincent in his *Word Studies* points out the same. He says St. Paul is thinking of the resurrection of the blessed. Evidently, then, there are two resurrections. One of these comes before the other, raising Christ committed men, and leaving the rest of the dead still in the grip of death's ghostly nakedness. The other, much later, raises small believing and unrepentant men for judgment.

Vincent notes several places where this tremendous idea comes to expression in the New Testament. One is St. Peter's great shout, in which he says Jesus' resurrection out from among the dead has begotten men anew, unto a living hope (I Peter 1:3). A second is St. Luke's description of the Gospel in *The Acts*. He says the apostles preached through Jesus the resurrection out from among the dead (The Acts 4:2). A third is the text.

This striking New Testament expression strongly supports what I have come rather recently to regard as a most glorious Gospel truth—the truth that Chris-

JESUS CHRIST IS LORD 125

tians do not die; that Christ omnipotently lifts them clear of death in the very midst of their mortal experience. Small believing men—atheists and secularists, the unrepentant—continue to die, just as they did before Jesus rose and ascended; but large believing men are lifted clear of death, and attain immediately to share with Christ His increasing reign above history.

Death for the Bible is never extinction, but a dark experience of being cut off from contact with the world of sense. Having died, men still have consciousness, memory, conscience, and a knowledge of such ideas and purposes as their telepathic powers enable them to come in contact with. They lose, however, the objective universe with all the wonder of its form and color. Jesus repeatedly used the expression "outer darkness" (St. Matt. 8:12, 22:13, 25:30), and I find myself wondering if He was not describing the lonely experience of the *small believing* dead.

Victory over death! Here is a truly immense conception. Death is a terrific violation of man's moral and aspiring life; and victory over it is one of the necessities of a moral universe. In the Bible's great redemptive hope it is the final goal—"The last enemy that shall be destroyed is death" (I Cor. 15:26).

The apostle asserts that Christ was the first fruits from the grave; and while there is some difficulty in harmonizing his statement with passages in the Old Testament, I am persuaded that it is true. Christ arose first, and then the multitude of the faithful dead, who had been waiting for His triumph, rose with Him.

How magnificently fitting it is that He, who was so wrongly humiliated upon the Cross, should be first to triumph over the grave!

The *Gospel According to Nicodemus,* an apocryphal writing of the early second century, actually describes the Saviour's leading of faithful men, who had lived and died before the Incarnation, out of the place of the dead. Indeed the new Standard Revision similarly translates a statement of St. Paul's in Ephesians 4:8 —"Therefore it is said, when He ascended on high He led a host of captives, and gave gifts to men." There is also an item in the Gospel according to St. Matthew which at least suggests the same thing. It is the statement that graves in the neighborhood of Jerusalem were opened at Jesus' death; and that at His resurrection people came out of them and appeared to their loved ones in the city. This might very well be an unconscious witness to the rising of that multitude of faithful men at the time of Jesus' resurrection (St. Matt. 27:52f). There is a third New Testament reference, even more obscure. It is St. Peter's statement that Jesus preached to spirits in prison (I. Peter 3:19). Putting, then, all these statements together, along with the direct teaching of Jesus, which we will survey in a moment, we are inclined to the opinion that Christ was the first to rise from the dead; that He caused to rise a multitude of faithful men at His resurrection; and that since His resurrection all those who are related to Him by faith, are lifted completely clear of death.

Jesus' own teaching at this point is very explicit.

He said to the men of Galilee, who had shared His sign of the feeding of the five thousand, that His life was heavenly bread in a sense the historic manna was not. He cried to them, "Your fathers did eat manna in the wilderness, and are dead. This is the bread which cometh down from heaven, that a man may eat thereof, and not die" (St. John 6:49-50). Again He said to the multitude in Jerusalem at the Feast of Tabernacles, "If a man keep my sayings he shall not by any means die unto the ages" (St. John 8:51). And yet once more, standing with Martha in front of Lazarus' tomb, He said, "He that believeth in me, though he were dead, yet shall he live; and whosoever liveth and believeth in me, shall not by any means die" (St. John 11:25-26).

Here are three strong and explicit passages; and there are others which support the Saviour's clear meaning, showing that the immediate resurrection of believing men was firmly held in the primitive Church. Thus St. Paul says, "Christ . . . hath abolished death, and hath brought life and immortality to light through the Gospel." Again, in his second letter to the Church at Corinth, he describes in detail his eager hope to be clothed upon, and so never experience death's lonely nakedness (II Corinthians 5:1-3). Indeed I am inclined to the opinion that he thought of the rapture of the Church as a long process, which began with Jesus' resurrection-ascension, and would be completed at the end of history in the raising of living believers to meet the Lord in the air (I Thess. 4:16-17). The same would be true also of the First Resurrection, so called, as described in *The Revelation*—it was a long process, crowned with a dramatic climax (20:4).

We come here upon a new idea. It is that many of the great events of history are first a lengthened process, and then a dramatic climax. This is true of the second coming of Christ, as we will see when we discuss the Millennium. It is true also of the rapture of the Church, and of the Resurrection. The fact is most historic movements combine these two characteristics. The moral debacle of Germany under Hitler had been developing for full a hundred and fifty years. It began in the rationalism of the universities. It took a long stride forward through the influence of materialistic evolution and Ernst Haeckel's *Riddle of the Universe*. It became a dramatic climax in Hitler's program of world conquest, and liquidation of those he did not appreciate. The concentration camps and extermination chambers of Europe would never have developed apart from the rationalism and scientific determinism which preceded them. Long process with dramatic climax are thus everywhere the order of history; and we should not be surprised if they appear also in the Bible's great redemptive expectation.

If, however, this point of view seems difficult, one can unify the Biblical teaching concerning death and the resurrection by assuming that resurrection for the blessed takes place in two stages: one in the midst of their mortal experience, and one at the end of history. But whatever hypothesis one adopts to unify Scripture, it is evidently not sound exegesis to ignore the explicit teaching of Jesus upon this subject. Nor

JESUS CHRIST IS LORD 129

can we escape from our difficulty by calling in question the accuracy of St. John's report. In the Synoptic Gospels also Jesus repudiates death, though not with the discriminating exactness of His teaching in the *Fourth Gospel* (compare St. Matt. 22:31-32).

And so Jesus did evidently teach an immediate victory of *large believing* men over death, a victory which was omnipotently given to them in the very midst of their mortal experience. Furthermore, the primitive Church understood Him to have taught thus; and we find His teaching reflected in theirs. But there is one serious objection to this understanding. It is that the vivid facts of sense experience weigh heavily against what Jesus taught. *Large believing* men do evidently die, the same as *small believing* men; and those glorified bodies with which we like to believe they are clothed upon in the very midst of their mortal experience, simply do not appear.

Quite beyond possibility of question, this is true; and the probability is that this seeming contradiction between teaching and fact is what led the Church to tone down the teaching of Jesus. The difficulty, however, is not as great as it seems, for sense experience is not the sure criterion of reality we have imagined it to be.

In the first place, reality is not a solid frame, but instead an appearance produced by the continuous play of forces. To illustrate, the flash of lightning is the end resultant of a discharge of electrical tension, picked up by the human eye, recorded on the human brain, and experienced as light by the human mind.

In the second place, a very large part of the forces operating about us in the universe are quite beyond the range of man's sense powers. We see and hear and smell only in part. Du Nouy, in his *Human Destiny*, says we experience only a fraction of the reality that is continually being produced about us. The moth hears sounds, the eagle sees objects, the dog smells odors that are completely beyond our range. A vivid illustration of this is the radio. At any moment, and almost anywhere, hundreds of tunes could be heard if we had ears to hear them. But the radio wave is far beyond our range. We can hear pulsations from a fraction of a centimeter to a meter long. To every pulsation longer or shorter than these we are deaf. The radio receiving instrument translates the longer pulsations to our range, and so we hear them. So universally recognized is this principle that the late Thomas A. Edison before his death actually began exploration in an effort to invent a receiving instrument that would bring heavenly voices within our terrestrial range.

Reality, then, and our sense perception of reality, are widely different values. The universe is vastly more complex than we experience it; and it is entirely possible that the resurrection body may be developed before our very eyes, and we not see it. The fact is we know this experientially. The general residents of Jerusalem did not see the risen Christ. Spiritually prepared and specially equipped witnesses alone beheld Him. Joan of Arc alone saw the angel standing under the oak tree. Her companions neither saw him nor heard what he said. Joan both saw and heard him; and this experience and others which followed it equipped her to command the captains of France and to lead her armies to victory.

It is not learned but merely obtuse to call in question this larger range of reality which the new science of Parapsychology is now exploring. Our present probationary sense powers are only a preparatory equipment; and when they are enlarged at the resurrection, we will discover a vastly enriched universe. The visions so often given to *large believing* men at the threshold of mortality are illustrations of just how our natural sense powers are enlarged. Our passing saints do see visions that other men cannot see; and among these vsions is the sight of those glorified bodies —angels and men—that are completely beyond the range of our present sense perception.

I infer, consequently, that since man's sense powers do not bound reality, it is entirely unwarranted to assume that *large believing* men are not equipped with glorified bodies in the very midst of their mortal experience. Jesus definitely promised to lift those who belonged to Him clear of death, and we are completely safe in assuming that He fulfills His promise.

The fact is Jesus re-expressed this precious promise on the very night before the Cross. He said to His disciples that He was going away to prepare a place for them; that immediately He would return in the Resurrection; and that, then, after a time, He would come and receive them unto Himself. The break in Jesus' thinking in this conversation takes place between His announcement of His return in the Resurrection, and of His later coming to receive His disciples to Himself. Jesus indicates this break by the use of *and*. In Caesar's celebrated message to the Roman Senate there was no break in his thinking, and so he used no conjunction. He wrote, "I came, I saw, I conquered." They were staccato announcements of events that followed each other in rapid succession. Jesus' announcement to His disciples on the night before the Cross were in part the same. He said, "I go, I come," and then there was a break. He concluded, "and I will receive you unto myself." It is with such an enraptured homecoming that Jesus has replaced for those who trust Him the ancient gloom of death (compare St. John 14:1-3).

Not long after this promise was given, St. Stephen had the opportunity of trying it out; and the event completely fulfilled the expectation. In one moment his consciousness had been of stones bruising his body, and of multiplied pains. Then in the very next moment the sense of pain faded out, and in its place he saw a shining vision. The radiant Christ appeared in the midst of cloven skies, welcoming him into Eternal Life. Stephen addressed this Christ with a prayer of compassion, and was gone. His murderers probably dragged his body away, still identifying him with it; but Stephen in Heaven was quite through with that bruised flesh. His resurrection body would be in expressive identity with it; but apart from this historical relation, he left it completely behind him.

I have been in contact with many experiences

which closely reproduce this triumph of St. Stephen. Here is one of unusual beauty because of the particular circumstances in which it was set. A distinguished Philadelphia physician had a wife who had long been a member of the Christian Church. Often she had invited him to share its worship with her; but he had steadily refused to do more than maintain an occasional and casual contact. Her health had been frail. Indeed it was only his devotion and skill that had kept her alive. Then one winter she was taken with the flu. He nursed her with utmost care, their daughter also assisting him. At last she seemed to be on the road to recovery. And so one morning she conceived the idea that she would ride with her husband as he made his professional calls. Accordingly she asked their daughter to dress her in her fur coat and rubbers, and going down into the office waited for the doctor to return with the car.

After a little while he came, and was astonished to see his wife sitting in the office. He exclaimed, "Why Anna, what are you doing here,"

"I'm going to ride with you on your calls," she replied.

"You are going to do nothing of the kind," he said. "You are going back to bed and stay there till you are much stronger."

"O Dad!" she answered, "I feel so much better. I want to ride around with you like we used to do."

"Not this morning, Anna," he said; and with that he helped her back to bed. He took off her out-door clothes, and giving her a strong heart stimulant, tucked her in the blankets.

Just as he finished attending his wife, the telephone rang. It was the family next door where the father was dying. They wanted the doctor to come right away. Telling his wife to stay in bed, and that he would soon be back, he went to attend the dying man. He was not gone long; and when he returned he came immediately to his wife's room. Entering it, he was amazed to see her sitting at the window, with a radiance in her face that quite transfigured it.

Completely astonished, he exclaimed, "Why, Anna, you're well. There's been a miracle!"

He did not believe much in miracles; but her face was so transfigured his immediate thought was of health, vitality and a supernatural cause. He exclaimed again, "Why, Anna, you're beautiful! I always knew you were good to look at, but never so beautiful as I see you now!"

His wife made no reply to either of his exclamations; but just sat there with fixed gaze and radiant The doctor went over to look at her more closely; and then he knew that she was passing. Almost as this conclusion dawned within his mind, she went.

I preached at that devoted woman's memorial service, and buried her body; and then soon afterward on Maundy Thursday, I went back to have a heart to heart talk with the doctor.

He said, "Preacher, I have often heard you say on the air that Christians do not die; that in the very midst of their mortal experience they are clothed upon with Eternal Life. I used to think you had exaggerated in those beautiful stories; but now, having seen my wife pass, I know you did not. I have seen death many, many times, and I know what it looks like; and I tell you my wife did not die. She sat there with a radiant face, gazing into the glory; and then after she knew that I had seen her, she went out into it."

"No, doctor," I responded, "your wife did not die. She sat looking into the glory of God; and then went out into it. She waited for you to see that glory in her face before she went. It was her climactic call to you. It is Maundy Thursday; and tonight at the Church you will make answer to her call, publicly confessing Christ, and uniting with His Church."

"It's too late," said the doctor, "for now she'd never know, even if I should do it."

"You're mistaken," I replied, "she will know. She knows everything we have just said to each other; and she's eager for you to respond to this, her supreme call."

"I can't make any promise," said the doctor.

"I didn't ask you to make a promise," I responded. "I merely told you your wife will know, and that you will respond just because you can't say, No, to this supreme call."

That night the doctor was at Church, and made his public confession of Christ: and from that Maundy Thursday service forward he was present at every service of public worship as long as I knew the church. He did even better. He became an active Christian witness telling all his patients how enriching the experience of relation to Christ was, and how much he received from his regular attendance upon public worship.

It is hardly necesssary to say a single word to enforce the point of this noble story. The elevation of his wife's passing was so great it completely commanded the doctor. The glory in her face made it radiant. The impression was so strong that the doctor thought she was supernaturally well and vital. Afterward he marvelled at her extraordinary beauty, exclaiming about it. Only at the very last did he realize his wife was dying, and that the radiance in her face was a reflection of the infinite glory upon which she was gazing. That the doctor could be thus commanded by truths which up to that time he had hardly believed, speaks for itself. It shows that the Christian's passing from this world can be an experience of such elevation as quite abolishes death. And this is precisely the Biblical promise—*large believing* men do not die. In the very midst of mortality they make contact with all the nobilities in which they have believed, and go forth exultantly into perfect and infinite fulfillment.

As we sit in the glory of this climactic experience, I would like to add some short paragraphs summarizing the redemptive service of Jesus Christ.

At the end of His public ministry, He was, as He, Himself, describes it, "lifted up" in the experience of the Cross, the Resurrection, and the Ascension.

In His rising, He raised with Himself, a multitude of faithful men, who had been awaiting His great victory.

Restored to the glory of His Father, He commanded the Holy Spirit upon men to abide.

Reigning, now, above history, He lifts believing men clear of death, in the very midst of their mortal experience.

He welcomes them to His presence, inviting them to share with Himself the increasing conquest of history. This redemptive toil must continue until every enmity has been overcome.

Returning at the end of history to establish judgment, He will bring this victorious company with Him, transforming the Church then alive upon the earth into the same glory.

At that time He will raise the multitude of *small believing* dead for judgment, equipping also the *small believing* living for the same experience.

He will then establish judgment, making a final end of sin—both demonic and human.

Then, climactically, He will carry up the redeemed and perfected human race into the glory of God. Being their Head, He will even share man's destiny with him.

Thus He will complete God's cosmic poem, crowning creation with a holy society, which is both Christ enriched and Christ guided.

Glory be to the Father and to the Son and to the Holy Ghost, as it was in the beginning, is now, and ever shall be, world without end. Amen.

THE CONSUMMATION WITHIN HISTORY

I Corinthians 15:25

"For he must reign until he has put all enemies under his feet."

The Scriptures anticipate two consummations—one within history, and one beyond history. The consummation within history has come to be called The Millennium, because the prophecy is that it will endure for a thousand years.

St. Paul in the text fore-visions this consummation within history. He says, Christ must reign within history until He has brought all enemies under His feet (I Cor. 15:25). Of course Christ's reign has already begun; and Jesus, Himself, announced the same, exclaiming to His followers, "All authority is given unto me in heaven and in earth" (Matt. 28:18). Evidently "in heaven" means above history, and "in earth" means within history. Consequently, Christ's reign began with the Resurrection-Ascension, and the Millennium will just be a period within history when His kingship is magnificently recognized.

As a matter of fact, the New Testament has very little to say about the Millennium. Jesus did indeed teach that the Kingdom would expand like the growth of corn—"First the blade, then the ear, then the full corn in the ear" (Mark 4:28). He also spoke of the Son of Man making an entrustment to His servants on which they would report at His return (Luke 19:12). There is also in *The Revelation* a description

JESUS CHRIST IS LORD

of the increase of the Kingdom down the centuries, and of its consummation during the Millennial Age. It is, however, to the Old Testament one must turn for the details of the Millennial expectation.

Thus Isaiah tells us that the Kingdom will be organized around the person of Messiah (11:1); that it will be an era of righteousness and peace (11:2-9), and that the people will live to a great age in it, the mortality of children being practically eliminated (65:20-22). The Prophet Malachi, also, teaches approximately the same (3:1-6). A number of prophets foretell that Israel will dwell securely in her own land; and that in the influence of her high faith will reach out into all the world (compare Isaiah 35:4-10; Daniel 7:13-14; Isaiah 65:23; Micah 4:1-7).

One could considerably multiply such details; but these are sufficient to establish the main outline of prophetic expectation. The important matter is to notice that this temporal consummation is both relative and of brief duration. Both death and birth continue during its progress, both probation and sin. Indeed this temporal consummation is a probationary and redemptive value simply. It cannot be compared with that perfect Kingdom which is the glory of the eternal ages.

This distinction we are making between the relative and the perfect, the temporal and the eternal, the historical and the celestial is most important; and the Millennium belongs to the former of these two classifications. The great final consummation in heaven stands thus quite alone. Nor should we allow ourselves to be confused with respect to this discrimination. The relative can approach the perfect, but it never can attain to it. Thus, the relative always leaves room for some degree of uncertainty with respect to God. The perfect does not do this. In the perfect world God will become a certainty, a commanding presence, and sin will have become a complete impossibility.

During the continuance of the relative, however, human societies will have uniformly a three division characteristic; that is the populations will freely divide themselves into three general groups—(1) The morally and spiritually committed; (2) The morally and spiritually uncommitted, who do nevertheless conform; and (3) The morally and spiritually uncommitted, who are in actual rebellion against any moral order. When the first of these groups is firmly established and large, the second group also will tend to be large, and the third group will be negligible. When, however, the first of these groups is either poorly established or small, the second group will be greatly diminished, and the third group will become large and threatening.

This is precisely what happened to England during the blight of Deistic philosophy. Commitment at the moral top of society was faltering; and as a consequence, the merely conformed group was greatly diminished. It tended to disappear; whereas the rebellious group became large and threatening. The records of 18th century show that there was great lawlessness in the England of that date; that more than a hundred and fifty crimes had death as their penalty; and that in spite of this severity, law could not be enforced. Free government was well nigh unfounded.

The Millennium, as a world era, will be one precisely opposite to the era produced by Deism. The convictions and purposes of the top moral group in society will be both broadly founded and firmly fixed. Their virile influence will build a large conforming group, which, while they will remain uncommitted, will nevertheless be conformed. The rebellious group, which is neither committed nor conformed, will be extremely diminshed.

Strikingly enough, it is precisely thus that *The Revelation* describes the Millennium. Satan will be bound, not eliminated. and the great peace will last only a thousand years, not forever. At the end of this period Satan will be released and will again betray the nations into war. Manifestly, unless the binding and loosing of Satan are to be conceived fantastically, and not as moral circumstances, his binding must result from a tremendous moral concensus, and his loosing from a great reduction of that consensus. Having seen the 19th century, which Professor Latourette rates as the supreme century of faith, succeeded by the twentieth, we can understand the possibility of this tragic oscillation of the centuries between high self-commitment, and blighting self-assertion.

In any event, such is the prophetic expectation. The Millennium is a consummation within history, and will be produced by historic forces within the probationary frame of experience now familiar to us. It will be a period of great but relative good, which having endured for a thousand years, will be succeeded by a new and aggravated era of world evil.

Confronting this expectation, and remembering how radically the Christian Church has already transformed civilization from the crude brutality of the pagan order which preceded it, we do not find it difficult to imagine our present age being succeeded rather swiftly by the accomplishment of the prophetic age of peace.

For example, imagine both the Church and the University as becoming completely dedicated to the truth of God, to the dignity of life, and to righteousness! Such a dedication, broadly established, will influence both life and civilization superlatively. This single accomplishment will have literally incalculable effects upon the moral and spiritual consensus of society.

Then, again, imagine the creative results that would follow from it if a substantially universal observance of the Lord's Day could be achieved. What elevation of the public mind! What poise both of body and mind would result!

Or, once again, conceive the consequences of a cultural improvement of the radio and television programs! Or of the achievement of an intellectual sensitiveness which would make men generally readers of informing Christian literature. We can get a suggestion as to the fruitfulness of this latter accomplishment from what it actually achieved in England under the leadership of John Wesley.

Then conceive the achievement of universal peace through the leadership and authority of such a super government as the United Nations. Such a government cannot, indeed, achieve "the peace of God", but it can accomplish a policed peace—the kind of peace we now enjoy in our several municipalities. The social consequences of these changes would again be quite incalculable. To begin they would reduce taxation by better than one-third, and this would have far reaching social significance.

Finally, add to all these other changes the consequences that can result from society's ability to take full advantage of the fruits of applied science—its replacement of our former economy of scarcity with a new economy of abundance, its annihilation of distance, isolation, etc., the results of these changes must necessarily be immense. They can, in fact, make it possible for modern men to eliminate, or at least to bring under social control practically all the ancient scourges of his organized life.

Confronting these now easily possible accomplishments of Christian civilization, I affirm it is not visionary to conceive the almost immediate appearance of a new and higher civilization. The work can be done; and if it is accomplished it will realize every Biblical promise with respect to the great prophetic age of peace. Of course Christ and His glorified saints will be reigning in such a world, only their thrones will not be visible on earth. They would be established above history, which is manifestly the plane at which Christ's own throne has been established from the

Ascension forward.

We must be careful here, for many Bible students have long anticipated a visible reign of Christ on the earth during the age of peace. Clearly, however, this anticipation must be mistaken, for it would involve a confusing of *time* with *eternity*, and of the *relative* with the *absolute*. There are several circumstances which are definitely characteristic of time, which are completely excluded from *eternity*. Thus in *time* God and the transcendent is partly revealed, and partly concealed; and this partial concealment is necessary in *time,* if probationary man is to remain capable of saying, "No," to God. As soon as God and the transcendent become certainties, they begin to exercise a coercive authority over probationary man, and so to terminate his probationary experience.

Again, probationary freedom pre-supposes a certain right of the free man to choose wrongly, but no such freedom belongs to *eternity*. In *eternity* all possibility of wrong will have been excluded by the completed free commitment of every individual person to the righteousness of God. *Time* is thus markedly different from eternity; and it is a serious confusion of thinking when we mix the two.

But there is yet another reason why the understanding of the Millennium we have been developing is necessary to the Biblical point of view. It is that for the New Testament, the Second Coming of Christ —His great climatic coming—is always presented as introducing the final judgment. Thus:

Christ says He will confess and deny men at His

JESUS CHRIST IS LORD

Coming (Mark 8:38). He says, again, that He will condemn at His Coming unprofitable servants who have wasted their talents (Luke 19:28). He says, once more, He will exclude from the marriage supper those virgins who have allowed themselves to run out of oil (Matt. 25:11). Then, more explicitly still, He says He will divide men right and left at His Coming, and that some will go away into everlasting punishment, but the righteous into life eternal (Matthew 25:31ff).

Similarly, the epistles steadily anticipate judgment at the Coming, and aspire to be found blameless. Such expressions are almost a refrain in the epistles (compare I Thess. 313, 5:23; I John 2:28; I Peter 1:13). St. Paul even describes the *Coming* as the revelation of the Lord Jesus from heaven "in flaming fire, inflicting vengeance upon those who do not know God" (II Thess. 1:4-10), and slaying the "Lawless One with the breath of his mouth" (II Thess. 2:8).

The fact is *The Revelation* itself, in the classical Millennial passage, seems to teach this same conception of the Coming. It describes, first, Christ's conquest of the ages, as at the head of His white robed host He rides down the centuries, the great sword of His Word issuing from His mouth. Manifestly, this action takes place above history, not within history; for no one has seen on earth, or will see on earth, this glorious array.

The description of this conquest, however, continues until the Beast (world evil), the False Prophet (his mouthpiece), and Satan himself are all taken.

World Evil, and his mouthpiece, the False Prophet, are cast into the lake of fire. Satan is only bound for a thousand years, and will be loosed at the end of that time. Then Thrones are made manifest, and the victors of faith are seen upon them. They are reigning with Christ (The Revelation 19:11-20:4). Nothing, however, has been said about Christ's coming in connection with these events. He still appears to be reigning above history. He has not yet been made manifest within it.

When the thousand years are past, Satan, released from his chains—that social consensus of truth and righteousness which has bound him—once again deceives the nations. The result is a defiant war not only against God's servants upon earth, but also against God, Himself. This is the maturity of the "Man of Sin" (II Thess. 2:1-12), and heaven's response to it is both instant and fully decisive. In *The Revelation* Christ is not mentioned, but fire does fall from heaven to decide history's climatic battle. In St. Paul's account of the same event fire comes out of Christ's face at His Coming to destroy the "Man of Sin."

Confront now the importance of this Biblical truth of a consummation within history before the great final consummation which is above and beyond history. In the first place this truth fits the nature of probationary man, who finds heaven too diverse from earth to command his full devotion. Probationary man really needs to feel the pull of something closer to life as he now knows it. It is because men do feel this

JESUS CHRIST IS LORD

need and feel it urgently, that Communism can fling its dishonest jibe at Christianity that it only promises *pie in the sky by and by*. Christianity's Millennial promise is the complete answer to this shallow falsehood; but the point I am making is that the Communist jibe has appeal just because men do feel the need for a near consummation, one within history, as well as that great ultimate consummation beyond history.

And the Church's glorious reforming record has been working toward the fulfillment of this great longing of men's souls, as well as toward the noble Biblical promise. The Kingdom has indeed been expanding, expanding most gloriously. It has both girdled the earth with faith, and deeply changed the character of its civilizations.

The Martyr Church had not yet won its legal right to exist within the Empire when it began to change pagan civilization. It rescued cast-off infants from the city streets where their pagan parents had abandoned them. It treated women with a new respect that pagan society had never accorded them. It promoted the manumission of slaves. It refused any recognition whatever to the bloody games which were the chief amusement of the Empire. It did all of this, and abundantly more. The truth is that the reforming influence of Christianity upon social institutions has been so immense that few men have any realization of its grandeur. In contemporary Communism the human individual is little better than a rat; and he was little better than a rat in the days of the Empire. The slaves—half the inhabitants of the Empire—were literally without rights. They could not bring an action in the courts, nor could they bear testimony there except under torture. The modern sense of mankind's universal dignity is essentially a Christian resultant; and of course it is the foundation of that mighty social drive for free government which we know as the democratic movement. Democracy literally burst out of the heart of Christianity, and in particular it burst out of the heart of the Reformation.

Popular education also has the same origin, and so, too, has higher education. The Wesleyan Revival in particular was immensely fruitful of social reform: and the emphasis upon reform in the modern Church has been so extreme that it might be said to have become a dangerous exaggeration.

The idea, then, of a consummation within history, and produced by historic forces, is one that is characteristically Christian. We face now the time question. Have we any right to believe that the hour of this glorious accomplishment is near at hand?

In answer we set down an emphatic, Yes. New levels of civilization are uniformly the results of new forces developed within any age. Thus Modern Times displaced the Middle Ages when an accumulation of new forces made such a development necessary. Martin Luther only sparked and guided the explosion; he did not, properly speaking, produce it. Here are some of the forces involved:

Ancient learning had been coming to increasing recognition toward the end of the Middle Ages, and the Universities were maturing into a major and

JESUS CHRIST IS LORD

recognized social force.

The cities with their free guilds were also a growing social influence.

Then there were a number of great discoveries—the discovery of printing by movable type, the discovery of the Western Hemisphere, the discovery of the telescope, the replacing of Ptolmeian astronomy with Copernican astronomy.

Then, too, the Italian Renaissance with its emphasis upon culture to the exclusion of morals, increased the growing corruption of the Church into an intolerable scandal. Men resented the burning of John Huss. Men resented, too, the filling of Europe's most important ecclesiastical positions with papal bastards (called nephews).

Finally there was the open shame of the traffic in indulgences. Luther's Ninety Five Theses nailed to the door of the Castle Church (Oct. 31, 1517) was the the spark that exploded into united action all these forces. And so the Protestant Reformation burst with its immense emphasis upon Christian truth; and the modern age was born.

But is there now anything resembling a similar situation developed or developing? The answer, of course, has to be another emphatic, Yes. There are seven forces, all of them well developed, which makes it certain that a new age is again at the borning.

(1) First, there is the contemporary sharp reaction against the speculations of contemporary Scientific Determinism — Materialism, Naturalism, Behaviorism, and the rest. This reaction had been

sharpened by the evident fact that the brutalities of Naziism and Communism have had their common origin in these foundationless speculations.

(2) Paralleling this repudiation of scientific determinism has been the resurgence of Christian truth. This is the Neo-orthodoxy, which is effectively challenging determinism even on university campuses, and both in Europe and America.*

(3) The amazing advance of the physical sciences has vastly enriched the resources of the human race. It has greatly improved both travel and communications; and it has multiplied production until it has changed our former economy of scarcity into one of abundance.

(4) Paralleling all of these, and in part explained by some of them, is the awakening sense of dignity now characterizing the backward races. Literally millions of people in Asia, Africa, and the islands of the sea have come awake to the possibilities of life, and

---

*It is not necessary to accept the Neo-orthodoxy in its more extreme form as developed by Professor Karl Barth to appreciate its immense service to the Christian Faith. Some of the continental theologians have developed it quite differently; and so, too, has Professor Reinhold Niebuhr of New York. Personally, I am convinced that God is available to the natural man through His self-disclosure in the Gospels; nor do I admit those Gospels are anything like as undermined by Criticism as Professor Barth might be willing to concede. As I appreciate Criticism, it is only a subjective discipline, and very far from an exact science. However, the Neo-orthodoxy did spark, and has developed the contemporary intellectual reaction against Naturalism and Modernism, and by doing this it has rendered the Christian Faith an immense service. Its emphasis upon dialectical truth has opened up a great new theological point of view, which is indispensable to a complete understanding either of the Biblical revelation or of life.

are rapidly becoming literate.

(5) Then both the shrinking of our world, due to the airplane and the radio, and the discovery of the fission of the atom, have forced upon men generally a recognition of the awful costliness of war, and the inescapable need for a world organization that can guarantee justice and peace.

(6) All these developments are implemented by the facilities mankind now commands to carry on a program of world wide education—the radio, television, modern printing, and our greatly broadened human understanding.

(7) Finally, the continued threat of Russian Communism, with its dishonest, but none the less, arousing emphasis upon the inequality of wealth, is steadily making it impossible for free civilization to face with complacency existing social inequalities.

Every one of these seven forces has a driving potential at this hour. If they are operated by men inspired by Christian truth, the prophetic age of peace may very well become an early realization. If they are operated by men frustrated by a false belief in determinism or Communism, then the age of peace may well be thrust aside until the human race learns more deeply the inherent tragedy of small ideas.

Professor Arthur Schloessinger in a recent discussion of Whitaker Chambers' *Witness* expressed the fear lest America's growing hostility to Communism and to Scientific Determination might leave no room for the irreligious man. He quoted Mr. Justice Jackson to the effect that freedom of religion could not be maintained unless there was freedom also of irreligion. I do not differ from Professor Schloessinger and Justice Jackson; but I would make this serious point: *We must grant freedom to irreligion; but we ought to be aware, while we are doing so, that there is no possible way of avoiding the serious costliness of this grave necessity.* The small believing man is necessarily a social liability which large believing men and women must carry.

Here is a series of facts which illustrate this point. When Charles Darwin published his *Origin of Species* in 1859, Adam Sedgwick, Woodwardian Professor of Geology at Cambridge University, and a past president of the British Association for the Advancement of Science wrote to him as follows: "Many of your wide conclusions are based upon assumptions that can neither be proved or disproved . . . we all admit developments as a fact of history: but how came it about? . . . There is a moral and metaphysical part of nature as well as a physical. A man who denies this is deep in the mire of folly . . . You have ignored this link; and if I do not mistake your meaning, you have done your best in one or two pregnant cases to break it. Were it possible (which thank God it is not) to break it, humanity might suffer a damage that might brutalize it and sink the human race into a lower grade of degradation than any into which it has fallen since its written records tell us of its history" (Life and Letters, Vol. I, pp. 42-45).

What Darwin definitely did not do, Ernst Haeckel did. In his *Riddle of the Universe* he broke the link between secondary and final causes. He abolished God, and reduced the universe and man to mere purposeless accidents. Because Haeckel did this, and because Europe eagerly read his shallow speculations, a whole series of tragic consequences has happened in our modern world.

To be swiftly explicit, the ruthless brutalities of Naziism and Communism are dark fulfillments of the prophecies Adam Sedgwick made in his letter to Charles Darwin. In the concentration camps, extermination chambers, and wholesale murders of the last decades, the human race has indeed descended to a level lower than anything else recorded in its history. Can we assess the costliness of this adventure? It is something so terrible that it even helps us to appreciate the Cross. My point is that God did give to probationary man a certain right to be wrong. But that right cost God the Cross; and Ernest Haeckel's right to reduce aspiring man to the beast, has cost the free world a desolated continent, a frustrated Europe, and a piling-up of human woe beyond possible calculation. Was Haeckel's probationary freedom worth this much? The answer of course is, Yes: but this answer should only be spoken by one standing within the shadow of the Cross.

I conclude. The most majestic fact in consciousness is that of the free, holy, God. The second most majestic fact is that of free aspiring probationary man. To win free man from his proud self-assertion has cost God the Cross and man the piled-up tragedy of ages. We ought to remember this when we talk about the proper freedom of irreligion.

But God has a purpose, first within history, and then above and beyond it. We are facing an hour of immense possibilities in relation to God. With repentance, faith, and obedience the long foretold age of peace may be a possibility of humanity's immediate future.

AN INTRODUCTORY NOTE CONCERNING THE MILLENNIUM

Theology has long been familiar with two, and more recently with three attitudes toward the Millennium. These have been the Pre-millennial view, the Post-millennial view, and the A-millennial view. The first puts the great objective coming of Christ at the beginning of the Millennium, and makes it causal to it. The second puts that coming at the end of the Millennium, and makes it causal to judgment. The third, stumbles at the very idea of a Millennium, because it would be a violation of the order of history.

In recent years, however, theology has become aware of two ideas which completely resolve these differences of millennial interpretation, and make the three views one. These two ideas are those of redemptive action taking place above history, and of Christ's comings between the Resurrection-Ascension and Judgment Day, as multiple. Assuming the truth of these two ideas, it is easily possible to unify millennial expectation.

We start, then, with the truth that Christ and the

JESUS CHRIST IS LORD

victors of faith have been reigning above history from the Ascension forward, and that every crisis developed within history by His heavenly leadership will be a *coming*.

For this view the Millennium is a period of large faith, broad justice, and great peace achieved within history by Christ's heavenly leadership. Peace will be substantially universal, a condition which might now be realized if it were not for the intransigence of Russian communism. Christ has already released into our age so many new forces that their social potentiality can hardly be imagined. But the point I am making is that Christ has released them, and they mark off, according to His own use of the word, a *coming*. The circumstance that this *coming* leaves both Him and the victors unseen, demands no more elasticity in prophetic interpretation than He Himself made use of. But the important truth from the Pre-millennial point of view is that Christ's *coming* produces the Millennium, and this will be as true if His sovereignty is established above history, as if it were visibly manifest on the earth.

Beyond the Millennium there will be a new and defiant expression of evil. In proud self-assertion men will reject Christ's glorious authority. They will do this in spite of the fact that Christ's authority is now demonstrated as the spring of universal good. This defiant choice will be the evident maturity of the man-of-sin described by St. Paul; and it will call forth from heaven an equally manifest judgment upon itself. Christ will be revealed with the great company of the victors, the unrepentant dead will be raised for judgment, probationary history will end, and the living will be transformed. This stupendous dramatization of judgment will end time and bring in eternity just as the New Testament steadily affirms.

Such a Millennium, so initiated, so ordered, and so terminated does not violate history. It is of one piece with the rest of history, differing from it only because of the powerful historic forces Christ has released into probationary time. Because He has released these forces, and because believing men have responded to thm obediently, the Kingdom will be magnificently advanced. This advance will not be even yet the consummation of the ages—God's absolute goal—for sin will yet have its last wild fling, and Christ has yet to be made objectively manifest in a dramatic spectacle of judgment.

This point of view completely fulfills the A-millennial view, for it leaves history's order intact clear to the end of probationary time. It completely fulfills also the Post-millennial view, for it anticipates a climatic revelation of Christ to finish judgment and bring in the perfect purpose of God. But it fulfills also the Pre-millennial view, for it conceives the Millennium as resulting from one of Christ's intermediate *comings*, by which He and the victors who are reigning with Him will be established as the Lord of history—the author of an era of faith, of righteousness, and of universal peace.

I point out one further circumstance. Since all personalities will at last be made manifest before

Christ as the universal judge, there must be a *coming* beyond the Millennium, as the New Testament so continually affirms. Then every eye will see Him, and the unrepentant and unbelieving will shrink from before Him, fleeing out into the dark.

This point of view, which does make it possible to unify all interpretations of the Millennium, is that which is developed in the sermon which immediately follows.

The Author.

THE SECOND COMING OF CHRIST
Acts 1:11

"This same Jesus, which is taken from you into heaven, shall so come in like manner as ye have seen him go into heaven."

There is a widely accepted view, which holds that the apostles and even Jesus, Himself, expect the Saviour's almost immediate return to end history, and to bring judgment and the eternal purpose of God. With this view I find myself in part definitely unimpressed, and for three reasons.

First, St. Paul, whom it is asserted shared this expectation, certainly did not do so fully. He is quite definite that Christ cannot be made manifest in climatic judgment until after sin itself shall have become fully developed. Sin is, indeed, already working. The arrogant defiant "Man of Sin" is already with us; but he has not yet attained to express the full maturity of evil; and Christ will not be made manifest in decisive judgment until evil has become fully mature (II Thess. 2:1f).

Second, in Jesus' references to the future He sharply discriminates between near events, and far events; and all His prophecies deal with near events exclusively. As respects far events, those lying beyond the destruction of Jerusalem and the age of the Gentiles, He makes no fore-announcements. The fact is He is explicit that He does not know the time of His Second Coming. Consequently, He must have seen it as, rela-

JESUS CHRIST IS LORD

tively speaking, an event of the remote future (Matt. 24:24-36, Luke 13:32).

Third, all time beyond the Cross, the Resurrection-Ascension, and the gift of the Holy Spirit to abide is for the New Testament included within "Last Times"; nor is there any suggestion in the teachings of Jesus as to just how long these "Last Times" will continue. Our Lord, nevertheless says explicitly that they will be long enough to include a number of important developments—judgment on Jerusalem, the age of the Gentiles, and the preaching of the Gospel in the whole world. Some of these developments Jesus looked upon as *comings*, but they were not His climatic *coming*. The fact is He saw Himself as continuously coming from the event of the *Cross*, the *Resurrection-Ascension*, and the *Gift of the Spirit* forward.

During the Saviour's trial before the Sanhedrin, the High Priest formally adjured Him, saying, "Tell us if thou be the Christ, the Son of God"; and Jesus replied saying, "Thou hast said; nevertheless I say unto you, from this time forward ye shall see the Son of Man seated at the right hand of power, and coming in the clouds of heaven" (Matt. 26:63-64). The Greek, which we have translated *from this time forward*, is *ap arti*, and *from this time forward* is its exact force. The King James version's rendering, *hereafter*, is not the customary meaning of the words.

* Note on *ap arti*

In St. Mark's account of Jesus' response to the High Priest there is no time clause. Jesus merely announces that they will see Him seated at the right hand of power, and coming. St. Luke's account is different in form but is identical in meaning with that preserved in St. Matthews. Jesus says *apo tou nun*, which means, from this present moment on. The *new standard revision translates* it "from now on" (Luke 22:69, Mark 14:62).

Jesus evidently saw the events of His life surrounding the Cross as marking off a major epoch in history; and He saw all the crises of history which would follow these events as *comings*, or in the familiar apocalyptic language of the day, He saw them as manifestations of Himself as seated at the right hand of power, and coming in the clouds of heaven.

At least two of these *comings* are identified by Jesus—the Transfiguration, and another fairly near crisis, which suggests God's judgment upon Jerusalem.

The Transfiguration is designated explicitly as a *coming* in the *Second Epistle of Peter (1:16-18)*; and this identification is strongly suggested also by the context in which the incident is set in each of the synoptic gospels.

God's judgment on the Holy City is probably identified as *a coming* by these circumstances. It is an event that will take place within the life span of the then living generation (Matt. 24:34). It will take place, also, before the apostles will have completed their ministry to Israel (Matt. 10:23). Manifestly this near at hand *coming* cannot be the great *Coming* which is to end history and bring in the eternal purpose of God. It must therefore be some slightly remote, but yet relatively near crisis, which will interrupt the apostolic ministry to Israel. The great judgment on Jerusalem fits perfectly these designations.

After this interruption of the apostolic ministry to Israel, the preaching of the Gospel will go forward with such power that the Gospel will be carried to the whole world, and then at last the great *Coming* will be revealed.

This interpretation is not only effective for all the Gospel references, but it is strongly suggested also by *The Revelation*. In that mysterious book, immediately after the completion of judgment upon Jerusalem, which follows the sounding of the seventh Trumpet, there is a triumphant shout in heaven (11:17). Evidently the Revelator saw judgment upon Jerusalem as manifesting the expanding sovereignty of Christ, which is the force of Jesus' apocalyptic expression— "The Son of Man seated at the right hand of power, and coming in the clouds of heaven."

Doubtless if Jesus had looked more broadly down the centuries, He would have picked out many other comings which history would yet develop. The Imperial Edict of Toleration of the year 311 was such. So too was the completion of the conversion of Europe at the end of the first Christian millennium. The bursting of the Reformation in the year 1517 was also a *coming*, and the Wesleyan revival, the rise of the labor unions, the revelation of the fission of the atom.

Then, beyond all these *comings* will be the *Coming*, a *coming* that would be as definite and objective as the going away.

This emphasis upon the outward is at first surprising in view of the sustained inwardness of the New Testament: and beyond question the New Testament is characteristically inward. Nevertheless outward values are recognized as having significance. They correspond to and express inward values. They magnify inward values, and by doing so they contribute to the total wealth of reality. An inward value in outward expression is certainly a greater value than an inward value unexpressed. This is evidently the reason God chose to express His eternal glory in the poem of the universe. God magnifies His glory by expressing it; and we can see Him continually doing this all down the course of history. We will come to that a little later; but among all God's great expressions one would certainly expect to find the kingship of Christ over history included.

This is important, for modern men are so afraid of being anthropomorphic in their thinking that they are inclined to shy off from the great Biblical expressions of God's nearness to them. This truth, however, is powerfully presented, and it is a sustained point of view. Thus, Genesis describes man as made in God's image (1:26); The Acts conceives him as inhabiting God's infinite consciousness (17:28); Isaiah pictures him as receiving immense Divine self-disclosures (6:1-4); Ezekiel presents him as commanded to stand erect in the Divine presence (2:1). The Gospel of John portrays him as redeemed by a Divine incarnation (1:14), and then as called to share the innermost mystery of the Divine glory (17:24)—manifestly, if we are going to take the Biblical revelation seriously

JESUS CHRIST IS LORD

we cannot stumble at the idea of history at last expressing the utter supremacy and sovereignty of the Saviour.

History, we must remember, is an enduring value. It does not fall away into nothing behind us, as it seems to do. History endures in the perfected memories of men, as well as in the absolute all-knowledge of God. The past is always fully present to God, and because it is, a manifestation of the kingship of the incarnate Son at the climax of history must be seen both as a fitting and even as a sublime expectation.

From God's point of view history falls into two great periods, separated by the Incarnation. These two periods might be called *Preparatory Times*, and *Last Times*. During *Preparatory Times*—all time before the Incarnation, God was conducting a demonstration on a world scale of the insufficiency of self-sufficient man. That is He was demonstrating that man could not by his own natural powers attain to the destiny he visioned. Man can indeed dream great dreams, but he does not have the power to realize them. The Tower of Babel, which should reach to the sky, might be taken as a symbol of this whole period. Self-sufficient man wills to attain to God; but he cannot. He dreams world empire, he dreams free government. Plato even writes his *Republic;* but the building of these things was beyond man's powers. In spite of all his dreams the world before the Incarnation was a time of dark superstitions, almost continuous war, ruthless plunder, slavery, and hovering despair. Such ancient institutions as the professional mourners, the slave, the judicial use of torture, and the gladiatorial show express the depth of its tragedy.

Then in the midst of *Preparatory Time* God began His great approachment to man. He called Abraham, and gave to him as a covenant *the eternal law of salvation*. Man must end his flight from God, renounce his proud self-sufficiency, and attain to live continually in the Divine presence, being perfect by the standard of the Divine moral glory (Genesis 17:1).

Later came the institution of the Theocracy. God came nearer to men, actually dwelling among them under the symbol of His august Ten Words, and solemn sacrificial ritual.

Then from within the Theocracy God spoke to men through a succession of prophets. They delivered Divine oracles of judgment upon man's self-sufficient life and civilization. They concluded the whole world under judgment—Israel, Judah, the surrounding nations, the great world empires—failure was universal.

But the prophets revealed something else beside the failure of man. They revealed also the grace and sufficiency of the holy God. "The Lord our righteousness" was their exalted confidence. They foretold the coming of a great Messiah, whose very name was salvation—"Wonderful Counsellor, the Mighty God, the Everlasting Father, the Prince of Peace."

In this tremendous disclosure both of judgment and hope *Preparatory Times* came to an end. God had gained four redemptive values through it. He had demonstrated the inadequacy of self-sufficient man. He had revealed His moral glory. He had produced a national civilization that could conceive a Divine incarnation. He had fixed the hope of one nation upon Himself.

When these things had been accomplished, it was the "fulness of time," and God came superlatively near to men. He became incarnate. In a sense the Kingdom of God began with this stupendous Divine act, for from the Nativity forward God always had one perfect son alive within creation. In another sense the Divine Kingdom began with the gift of the Holy Spirit to abide—that is with the instituting of the God-indwelt community. In still another sense the Divine Kingdom began with the destruction of Jerusalem, that is when the God-indwelt community was set free from the restraints of Jewish formalism, and made effectively a world force.

Whichever date one accepts for the beginning of the Kingdom, the instituting of the Kingdom does commence the second great epoch of history—*Last Times*. Now God is demonstrating before all intelligencies the inherent creativity of the God-indwelt life and society.

And just as within *Preparatory Times* God began something new in the call of Abraham, so also within *Last Times* God again begins something new in the revelation of the Millennial Age. The God-indwelt life and society will necessarily bear fruit unto freedom and blessedness. In the forepart of *Last Times* God's demonstrations are partly negative and partly positive. Sometimes He is redemonstrating the tragic impoverishment inseparable from the self-sufficient point of view. Sometimes He is demonstrating the abounding good that is the necessary result of the God-indwelt experience. During the martyr age He demonstrated both, the one over against the other. In the Reformation and the Wesleyan revival He demonstrated the creativity of the God-indwelt experience. In the consequences of Deism, and again in the consequences of Scientific Determinism or Naturalism, He has once again demonstrated the impoverishment necessarily springing out of the self-sufficient point of view. The Millennium, of course, is the supreme demonstration of the abounding good which necessarily flows from the God-indwelt life and community. Evil will be sharply curtailed. Righteousness and peace will abound. Expanded freedom and human well being will be the glorious consequence.

Once again I say this exceeding nearness of God to men is not difficult to believe after we have cut ourselves loose from those human speculations by which man's pride of intellectual self-sufficiency has presumed to correct the revelation of God. God is not unknowable. He is eager to come near men. Man is not a mere pawn of cosmic forces. He is a free, rational, moral personality, whom the eternal Infinite invites into His presence. The pressing need of our age is to recover God's revealed Truth in all its dignity and grandeur, unconfused and undiminished by our human speculations—Dialectical Materialism, Scientific Determinism, Naturalism, Behaviorism. All these speculations are doubtless individual facets of truth exaggerated into absolute and all-embracing

JESUS CHRIST IS LORD

principles. But as thus exaggerated they become confusing falsehoods, which degrade and frustrate man, robbing him of his birthright.

And so the Bible looks forward to a consummation of the Kingdom within history, a time of great righteousness and great blessedness. There will be Godliness, there will be righteousness, there will be peace, and there will be abundance; and these things will be developed within history in interaction with Christ and His victors, who are reigning above history. Nor do these great expectations seem remote to me. Almost we could realize them now if we could but get completely free from the scourge of Scientific Determinism and the demonic arrogance of Russian Communism—but perhaps God needs to shake the free world with this threat a little longer until we add a few more to the Supreme Court's decision that American schools can recognize no racial distinctions.

But great as will be the blessing which will flow from this consummation of the Kingdom within history, man's pride will cause him to turn his back upon it. Again, as in the Renaissance, in Deist England, in the French Revolution, in Rationalist Germany, in the absurd self-worship of Western civilization generally, man will turn away from God. And this time he will not do it in confusion, for the demonstration of good in the Millennium will have excluded all uncertainty. Every intelligence will know that Godliness is the fount of good. But human pride, like demonic pride, will have its self regardless. There is a point of view from which to be supreme looks more attractive than to be obediently blessed. And so for pride men will reject Godliness. The great consensus of Christian truth will be attacked and undermined. Satan will consequently be released from the chains which have bound him, and will go forth again to deceive the nations unto war.

Impossible exclaims someone. I answer, Do we not see men continually doing things that are equally absurd? Men know both the falsehood and peril of the liquor habit, and yet they dare it. Men know the discomfort and dangers of the tobacco habit, and yet they dare it. Men know the tragedy and falsehood of pride, and yet they make choice of it. Of course there is no sense in any of these choices, nor in a hundred more that are made by men every day; but we make them. It is one of the demonstrations of the reality of our freedom. We are so free that we can do the absurd, when we know the wise, the wrong when we know the right. We read the shocking accounts of automobile accidents, and yet drive our cars dangerously. We see the frustrations continually resulting from immoral love, and yet heedlessly pursue the vanity of adultery. Yes, this is our freedom; and it can even turn our backs upon Godliness and peace after they have been demonstrated, and turn our faces to the vanity of pride and even war.

In this climatic choice of pride and self, sin will have become fully defiant. This will be the completion of sin. St. Paul's Man of Sin become mature. Man knowing the creativity of the God-indwelt life and community, but wanting instead to stand alone. Proud man really resents the humility of sonship's obedience. He would rather have less and be less, alone, than have all and be all, in a humiliating dependence upon the infinite Presence.

When sin has become, thus, conscious defiance, then God's judgment upon sin will become fully revealed. Christ will descend the skies in outward glory, and judgment will become as manifest as the sun. This will be the climatic *Coming*. St. Paul pictures Christ as made manifest in the midst of the whole multitude of His victors. The Church on earth is in a moment transformed into the same glory; and so again, as once before, two companies meet exultantly around Jesus' central figure. Long ago it was pilgrims from Galilee descending Olivet with Jesus, while a crowd from within Jerusalem ascended the mount to meet them. At the last it will be all the victors of the ages descending the skies with the glorious Christ, while pilgrims of earth, swiftly transformed into the same image ascend to meet Him in the air.

It will be a moment of completly unbounded rapture. No music that we now know will be adequate to express it—no, not even Handel's *Worthy is the Lamb*, or *Halleluiah Chorus*. Salvation will be at the very threshold of its full consummation. Sin will be at its utmost instant. Not to sing will be impossible. The very rocks would find voices if the tongues of men should fail.

The Revelation pictures fire as falling from heaven to bring to an end sin's final, mad assertion. St. Paul describes destruction as bursting from the very presence of Christ with overwhelming judgment. Jesus asserts that all nations will appear before Him, and that He will divide them right and left as a shepherd divideth the sheep from the goats.

As I conceive this solemn event, every man will be, as it were, clothed with his history. The immediate knowledge of telepathy will make each of us naked before God and all our fellows. Every act, every wish, and every motive will be made manifest. Even the most secret things will all be made known. Of course all proud assertive men will flee from such a disclosure; and of course all God-depending, repentant men will press eagerly into it. They will fall upon their faces, repudiating all that life had been. They will press forward to kiss the feet of infinite love, which having rescued them from tragedy, has glorified them to share the uttermost mystery of His eternal life.

Beyond this moral and dramatic climax the unbounded wonder of God's eternal purpose will lie open before the enraptured gaze of the innumerable Company. Now at last God will be satisfied. A unity of worlds, enshrining a unity of history and a unity of men will stand fully revealed. God's cosmic poem will be completed. Every falsehood of ancient sin will have been transformed by judgment into an expression of eternal truth. Every free creature will have become obedient to God's perfect all-embracing purpose: and so the universe will at last make one infinite music under the constant headship of the crucified, resurrected and enthroned Christ, who is both the leader and the fullness of an eternal salvation.

This, by and large, is and always has been the noble confidence of the Christian Church. This hope is fully affirmed in the New Testament, and confessed in the ancient creeds. The ages, thus, unite with the angels to affirm that "this same Jesus, which is taken from you into heaven, shall so come again in like manner as ye have seen him go into heaven."

THE CONSUMMATION BEYOND HISTORY
Ephesians 1:17-18

"That the God and Father of our Lord Jesus Christ, the Father of glory, may give unto you the spirit of wisdom and revelation in the knowledge of Him: the eyes of your understanding being enlightened, that you may know what is the hope of his calling, and what the riches of the glory of his inheritance in the saints."

St. Paul in this text is contemplating the mighty goal which is out beyond the creative ages. Jesus Christ crucified, risen, ascended is at the center of this goal. He belongs at once to the Trinity of God and to the redeemed race. Consequently, belonging to both solidarities, He welds them together by the uniting force of His person. So He, Himself, prayed: "And the glory which thou gavest me I have given them; that they may be one even as we are one: I in them, and thou in me, that they may be perfect in one."

Alfred Tennyson, walking abroad in England, saw one day a tender little flower growing between the rocks of an English crannied wall. He plucked the flower, root and stem and all, and held it in his hand. He wrote of it:

"Flower of the crannied wall,
    I pluck you out of the crannies;—
Hold you here, root and all in my hand,
    Little flower—but if I could understand

What you are, root and all, and all in all,
I should know what God and man is."

Tennyson saw the little flower as expressing an infinite mystery. What did it say?

Unquestionably its expression was manifold. To begin, it proclaimed a great unity. It was a unity within itself. It was a unity also with the earth and air about it. It was a unity once more with the sky above it; for making contact through its green leaves with the sun far away, it appropriated solar energy and transmuted it into growing plant life.

It was a unity, then, and as a unity it was creative. It had the power within itself both to grow and to bloom. In a faltering way this little flower could say like the Creator, "Let there be" . . . and it would be so.

Unity, creativity, and then third, service. This little flower fed the insects. They drank of its perfumed life. It fed also the animal world. Indeed it served even in its dying! For when it fell to the earth and disintegrated, the decay of its tissue became an enriching humus—the food of next year's growing.

And then the little flower had life. Life was a mystery; but the little flower had it. The poet was probably referring to this mystery when he wrote

"Little flower—but if I could understand
What you are, root and all ,all in all,
I would know what God and man is."

Unity, creativity, service, life and then immensity. The flower itself was so small that the poet could hold it in his hand: but its contacts were unbounded. It reached to the sun, and laid hold upon its mighty energy.

This was Tennyson's little flower. Its expressiveness was indeed majestic; but not quite as great as Tennyson imagined. Beyond the utmost meaning of the little flower there were still mysteries. There was the mystery of consciousness, the mystery of moral reason, the mystery of self-determination; and of these the little flower expressed nothing.

The flower in the crannied wall, then, does not have the total answer. It is just one line in the immense cosmic poem of God in which He proclaims the eternal mystery and glory of His life. Beyond the creation of that flower God went far, had to go far. He created man. He guided history. He became incarnate. He died and rose again, redeeming history; and only when all this shall be fully finished will God's cosmic poem at last be complete.

This, then, is the goal toward which creation is moving. It must express the glory of God. It must fully express Him to Himself. It must make answer to His Truth with truth, to His Holiness with holiness, and to His love with love. When creation has attained to do this, the creature will be beatified, and God Himself will be enriched. St. Paul in the text sees Christ as possessed of an infinite inheritance in redeemed humanity; and then he sees Him as sharing this inheritance with men, whom he describes as "the fulness of him who filleth all in all." God glorifies redeemed men; and as He does so, men make answer to Him, and their answer enriches the Infinite God.

JESUS CHRIST IS LORD

Having caught sight of the final goal, we now turn back to gaze upon some of its greater details, that we may appreciate their sheer immensity.

The fundamental meaning of God's life, and the fundamental motif of His cosmic poem is a great ascending crescendo of unity. God is one, and the universe also is one—a great revolving whole. We see this in Newton's principle. Gravitation is a vast attractive force which binds together all masses — worlds, atoms, and electrons. And just as God's all-embracing concern cannot lose one small sparrow from His case, so the all-embracing principle of gravitation cannot lose one electron, not even though it be out on the rim of the Milky Way.

Unity is thus the fundamental glory of God's life, and the fundamental emphasis also in God's cosmic poem. And then within this basic frame of unity, God has piled-up unities. Unities crowd creation. Every organism is a unity—plants, insects, animals, men. Just as Handel in the Hallelujah Chorus multiplied "halleluiahs," so God in His cosmic poem has multiplied unities. Every individual organism being a unity in itself, God has combined into larger wholes. So we have forests, swarms, herds, civilizations. And then still more complex, these groups are interdependent. Plants feed the animals. Insects fertilize the plants. Animal death promotes plant life: yes, and the disintegration of plant organisms becomes humus, so that the decay of last year's growth becomes the food of next year's growing.

At last at the summit God makes man in His own

image. He makes him free. He gives him the basic insights of moral reason. He enriches him with the sublime wealth of consciousness and self-consciousness. Man has the capacity of knowing, of knowing himself through all his other knowledge, and even of knowing God.

Here indeed is a summit; but it is not even so, *the summit*. There are reaches of creative activity beyond this in the great purpose of God. Man is not only an individual, he is a potential society, a civilization, a sweep of history; and all this had yet to be accomplished when God had finished creating the universe and man. Nor can God accomplish this total work alone. He has fashioned man so nobly that man himself must join in the further creative process. God is unquestionably the great willer; but man's small willing also is a necessity to the completing of the Divine purpose. It is like our great systems of electrical energy in which power flows outward from a central reservoir. That central reservoir does all the work; yet within every circuit is a trivial switch, which can either facilitate or prevent the flow of current from the reservoir. And precisely such is the relation of the creative freedom of man to the power of God. God could overwhelm man's small resources; but He will not; He respects them. He limits Himself to maintain them.

Unquestionably it was a costly adventure upon God's part when He made man free. Man's freedom involved terrific possibilities; but man's freedom was fundamental to every great thing God wanted to do.

Consequently, God dared the risk, and accepted the tragic results.

The great danger God confronted in creating man free, was not merely man's freedom, but the fact that this could be achieved only by giving to man a powerful sense of self. Man's sense of self had to be so powerful that it would make him independent of every other value—God, other people, circumstances, even his own intimate desires. Man had to be able to feel, *"I am I, sovereign, free, independent of everything which is not I."* But such a commanding sense of self can easily become life's dominating motive. When this happens man becomes self-driven; his desires all turn back upon himself; he worships self instead of God. This is the genius of evil, the particular choices in which it comes to expression are not significant. Self is on the throne, and whether it build a proud philosophy, a lordly dictatorship, or a petty greed, its consequences are equally damning.

So it was because of the enthronement of self that the universe went wrong. Self-centered men built chaos, not unity. They became tragic figures who could not express the glorious inclusiveness of God. And God foresaw these grave possibilities, but yet He carried through His purpose. He crowned His cosmic poem with free men. Then sin unfolded, as God had foreseen it would; and God stood the Incarnation in the midst of sin's mad confusion. Sinful men responded with a Cross; and God accepted even the Cross.

But notice, in accepting thus the Cross sin had

thrust upon Him, God overcame sin. In accepting the Cross God did three things. He, first, allowed sin to work its extreme malice upon Himself, advertising its innermost nature. He, second, expressed His redemptive love, by accepting in humble patience the bitter malice of the creature. He, third, judged sin, by displaying its extreme falsity before all intelligences, including the intelligence of those probationary sinners who would be moved to repentance by it. Having done this God was able to and did forgive all probationary sinners (those who sinned in confusion, not defiantly). He literally stood Himself thus a gazing stock in the midst of history, both judging, wooing and rescuing sinners. This is the imperishable meaning of the crucified and risen Christ.

Beginning with this one sublime, infinite life, a new movement spreads both forward and backward down the centuries.

Christ proclaims God's perfect salvation to a multitude of faithful men in Hades, who had been waiting for the completion of the Divine purpose.

The Spirit empowers a little group of men in Palestine to wait, to witness, and to die that this news of the Divine victory might be carried forward to the utmost reaches of existence.

These men become the Martyr Church; and the boundlessness of their devotion overcomes all opposition. The very word *martyr* is just the ancient word *witness* accented by their sacrifice. They witness and they die; but every dying witness multiplies himself. The blood of the martyrs is indeed the seed of the

Church. The elevation of their sacrifices is mightier than Rome's unconquered legions. The Empire surrenders. Emperor Galerius publishes the Edict of Toleration. Christ's Kingdom is an established force within history.

Seven centuries pass, and this heroic martyr witness has taken one continent in Christ's name. The work was not perfectly done; but it was none the less challenging. The Kingdom of God was now influencing one major section of the world.

Then the great Schoolmen made Christianity the accepted world-view of the West. From Anselm to Aquinas Christianity was made an all-embracing philosophy.

The Reformation followed; and Christian truth became not merely the accepted world-view of the West, but the intimately possessed knowledge of believing men and women generally.

This tremendous accomplishment issued in social reform piled upon social reform. The parliaments of free men succeeded the autocratic rule of kings.

Now, however, the great Reformation age is falling behind us, and a new age is coming to birth. The Gospel is once again today arrogantly challenged, but it has, notwithstanding, substantially girdled the earth. Evidently the forces are now available to bring in the prophetic age of peace.

There is still, however, much that God must do for redeemed men. The Spirit must complete their inward transformation, so that all of them are one within themselves. He must also continuously relate them to each other, so that every human relation is as perfect as the holy fellowship of God. Beyond this God must reclothe their perfect spirits with glorified bodies, completely freed from the limitations and decay of earth.

And at last, when all of this shall have been fully done, then the great climax of the Divine purpose will unfold, glorious as the rising of the sun. God's cosmic poem will be completed. The universe, which always has expressed God's oneness in its unity of worlds, will begin to express His holiness in its perfect human society. Men will live as free as God is free, and yet also as perfectly as God is perfect. Men will live with complete inclusiveness—each man in the life of every other one. We will reverence each other as we do both God and ourselves. Christ's intimately revealed presence will be a fellowship that will both energize and guide each choice. All understandings will be perfect. All relationships will be sublime.

It is impossible to imagine the rapture of such an experience. One can calculate its factors. One can set down its law in words much as scientists can write their mathematical equations; but to realize what these sentences mean in terms of actual life is quite beyond man's present powers. However, the whole multitude of the victors will at last be fully one. Great fellowship will cause souls to flow together as chords of music blend to become the wonder of an oratorio. It was for this very thing Jesus prayed on that last night before the Cross.

It is staggering! Incomprehensible! But we have

not even yet reached the summit. In the chapter from which we have taken the text the apostle speaks of the Church as being "the fulness of him that filleth all things." He thus seems to say that the Church is literally organized into the triune life of God. Christ fills the Church, glorifying it with His own glory; and the Church thus perfected and glorified is lifted up to become a constituent part of the eternal life of God. I heard Edwin Lewis say one day with a power of insight and expression that was thrilling, "God has modified forever the very structure of His eternal life to save lost men." And St. Paul seems to go even a step farther telling us that God has even incorporated redeemed men into the glory of His eternal unity. This is indeed the great Amen, which only at last in heaven our sin blemished humanity will be able to hear.

And so God's cosmic poem, advancing from a unity of worlds to a unity of men, will at last make answer to the holy God. It will make answer to His truth with its Amen, to His wisdom with its obedience, and to His Love with its humble, adoring, grateful human love. It will be a vast interaction, and it will be as inexhaustible as the glory of God. Forever redeemed men will explore the glory of the Divine Life. They will expore this as it is expressed about them in the majestic frame of the objective universe. They will explore this as it is revealed within them in the nobler majesties of the subjective universe—the universe of emotions, thought, truth, love. And every exploration will enlarge their knowledge, their understanding, their power to love, the grandeur of their grasp of truth, the depth of their expression of truth. It is completely inexhaustible, and because it is the heaven for which we wait must be as unbounded as the eternal life of God. One bows down overwhelmed with wonder. What Satan would have taken by spiritual violence, what he has urged man also proudly to assert, that God gives to the humble. It is like the mystery of romance. The love which a man seeks to take from a maid by force, but which she is utterly unable to give in response to that approach, she gladly bestows upon him who reverently woos her. So in *The Revelation* is recorded Christ's promise, "To him that overcometh I will give to sit down with me upon my throne, even as I also overcame and am set down with my Father upon his throne." It is the very summit of possibility. There is nothing higher that life can produce, or that thought can conceive.

EPILOGUE

"But when the Comforter is come, whom I will send you from the Father, even the Spirit of truth, which proceedeth from the Father, he shall testify of me; and ye also shall bear witness, because ye have been with me from the beginning."

The preceding chapters have surveyed the stupendous glory of Jesus Christ. But majestic as He is, He would long ago have been lost out of human knowledge—perished amid the waste of our vanished yesterdays, had it not been for the *Double Witness* which He provided. That witness is primarily the testimony of the Church to His sublime facts. Supremely it is the testimony of the Holy Spirit to His eternal glory.

This witness of the Church and of the Spirit is the power behind Christian civilization; and it is as essential to the ongoing of God's redemptive purpose as Jesus Christ, Himself. Whenever this witness falters, Christian civilization trembles. Could this witness wholly fail, Christian civilization would be completely unfounded.

But this witness will never fail: because, whenever it falters, men are so shocked by the social disintegration which results, that in humble repentance they immediately enlarge their witness. It is this circumstance which enables the Gospel recurringly to renew itself. This is the explanation of the Reformation's sudden rise in the midst of the moral chaos which followed the renaissance. This is the explanation of the Wesleyan revival's unfolding in spite of the spiritual debacle produced by Deism. This is the explanation of the contemporary resurgence of faith in spite of the continuing influence of our blighting naturalistic world-view. Men will follow the lead of a great falsehood only so far. When the edge of the abyss looms before them, inevitably they stop and ask themselves, What is the authority of these ideas which we have mistaken for Truth? It is because Arnold Toynbee has failed to note this deeply implanted resurgent power of the Gospel that the concluding volume of his magnificent work is so pessimistic.

The *Double Witness*, then, is not, and will never be a spent force. It has faltered, but it cannot fail. A new Reformation is even now in the making; and when it is fully developed it will sweep away before it the twin falsehoods of the twentieth century—naturalistic philosophy (often called scientific determinism), and imperialistic communism, as west winds sweep away the blinding mists of low hung fogs.

The Christian witness has been uninterrupted since the first Easter morning. Mary Magdalene, the other women, Peter and John were at the tomb that morning, and saw it was open and empty. They saw, too, the angels, who proclaimed Him risen from the dead. In these arresting events the witness began. Later it was enlarged by Jesus' personal manifestations. Those magnificent events created the first Lord's Day; and from that beginning forward there have always been Christian weekly assemblies to remember, to

JESUS CHRIST IS LORD

wonder, and to worship. These assemblies, this wonder, this worship is the unbreachable bastion of Christian civilization. It has nver been broken. It never will be broken. It has inspired what Dr. Halford Luccock so well describes as history's "unending line of splendor".

It will do us good with lingering gratitude to visualize this line. Not one century in the twenty since Jesus lived and died, rose and ascended, but is glorious because of those who served Him in it. During the martyr centuries there were the apostles—Peter, Paul, and John; and then the fathers—Papias, Polycarp, Justin Martyr, Irenaeus. At the opening of the third century Pantaenus, Clement, Hippolytus, Origen founded the first great Christian school at Alexandria. Other noble names of the third century are Cyprian, Tertullian, Dionysius, Gregory, Pierius.

In the fourth century the edict of toleration was proclaimed, and the Church came up out of its catacombs. It was the age of Constantine, the time of the Council of Nicaea. Its names in the "line of splendor" include Eusebius, Athanasius, Basil, Gregory, Ambrose.

From the fifth and into the eleventh centuries was the church's second period of missionary advance. During these centuries it took one complete continent in Jesus' name. The heroes of these centuries were Augustine of Hippo, Patrick of Ireland, Remegius of France, Ulphilias of the Goths, Brendan and Columban of Scotland, Augustine of England, Elegius of Belgium, Boniface the apostle and martyr of Germany, Anscar the apostle of Denmark, Alfred the great of England, Lanfranc and Anselm of Canterbury, Olaf Haroldsson king and evangelist of Norway.

In the twelfth century Bernard of Clairveaux was as the shining of a great light. In the thirteenth came sweet spirited St. Francis, and the great Dominican Thomas Aquinas. In the fourteenth Wycliffe, Eckhart and Tauler somewhat quickened men's souls. In the fifteenth John Huss, Jerome of Prague, and Savonarola spoke burning words and were martyred by a Church that had become apostate.

Then the Reformation burst with its galaxy of giants—Luther, Melancthon, Frederick the elector of Saxony, Zwingli, Calvin, William of Orange, Knox, Ridley, Latimer and Cranmer.

In the seventeenth century Fox founded the Quakers, and Gustavus Adolphus led his Protestant army to victory and martyrdom at Lutzen. The peace of Westphalia followed—the freedom of the Christian man's conscience was now politically established.

The eighteenth century was the era of the great revival. It was led by such glorious figures as Zinzendorf, Wesley, Whitfield, Edwards, George Handel, Sir Isaac Newton, George Washington.

In the nineteenth century the revival of the eighteenth came to social expression. It was led by Shaftsbury, Wilberforce, Livingstone, Gladstone, Abraham Lincoln, Phillips Brooks, Spurgeon, Finney, Moody, Booth, and Lightfoot.

And then came the twentieth century, a period of great confusion; and yet it too has produced notable names in the "unending line of splendor"—Crawford of Africa, Grenfell of Labrador, Olin Alfred Curtis, Henry C. Morrison, Robert E. Speer, Barth, Bruner, Schweitzer, John A. MacKay, John R. Mott.

These all alike have been humble witnesses to the glory of the fact of Christ—links in the tremendous chain of wondering devotion which has kept Him continually fresh, living, contemporary.

And this wondering worship which the Church has maintained unbroken from the first Easter forward is the indispensible pre-requisite of anything that can be called an advancing free civilization. Without these assemblies and this worship, high confidence in the dignity of life would inevitably have failed, and free civilization would have collapsed.

John Ruskin in one of his essays makes a classification of art, and sets off Christian art as a group by itself, superior to all other art whatsoever. As he saw it, Christian truth had lifted life to a new high level both of conception and skill which made new attainments in expression possible. And evidently Ruskin's insight is correct, for where in pre-Christian expression can one find anything to compare with Handel's *Hallelujah Chorus*? And where in pre-Christian poetry can one find anything that approaches the high confidence of Browning's *Saul* or Tennyson's *In Memoriam*? Or, to take expression in painting, concerning which Ruskin particularly spoke, where can one find in pre-Christian times a face to match the mingled strength and beauty of Jambor's "Christus", or Raphael's "Sistine Madonna"?

Yes, manifestly, the whole level of human expression has felt the impact of Christ as His sublime figure has been kept forever alive and contemporary by the power of the *Double Witness*. Greek architecture is serenely beautiful, but no architecture is as aspiring as the Gothic cathedral. Roman law was magnificently strong, but no government ever combined orderly strength with a recognition of the freedom and dignity of the individual as Christian democracy now does. It is even a serious question whether the natural sciences could have achieved their wonderful discoveries if the *Double Witness* had not first established men's confidence in the goodness and dependability of the universe.

The Christian witness is thus indisputably history's most significant value. That great cry which Jesus uttered shortly before the Cross — "And I, if I be lifted up, will draw all men unto me" — is a sure answer to every problem which civilization develops. Always, when men are given to see His figure in its unreduced dimensions, and its unbounded sweep of meaning, they are inspired. "The risen Christ, made forever contemporary by the believer's worship and th Holy Spirit's revelation" is indeed the answer to every need of life. The atom bomb is only threatening because so many men do not share in the inspiration of this high vision. Let the wondering worship of Christ become universal, and the atom bomb will immediately cease to be fearsome, indeed, it will cease to be significant.

And so Jesus Christ is Lord. He is Lord by virtue of that which He eternally is; but His Lordship can be socially effective only in so far as it is witnessed, appreciated, affirmed. Thus the unending line of witnessing worshippers, becomes historically as significant as the risen Christ Himself. Confronting Jesus' arresting words spoken to the apostles after His resurrection — "As the Father hath sent me, even so send I you" — Professor Curtis used to say, that as Jesus in His day carried the total responsibility for the progress of redemption, so the apostles did as the successors of Jesus, and the worshipping Church as the successor to the apostles. Christ in His death and resurrection perfected salvation; but within history this salvation is continually conditioned by the effectiveness of the Church's worshipping witness. When we believing men neglect our part of the great Divine-human interaction, God's part becomes impotent. We are but witnesses, the insignificant switch that conditions the flow of some mighty electrical current. But when the insignificant switch is wrongly turned, all the surging power of the mighty current becomes meaningless. And it would be the same if man's worshipping witness to the glory of the risen Christ were allowed to fail—all that redemptive sufficiency which is complete in Him, would, so far as history is concerned, become as if it had never been.

www.ingramcontent.com/pod-product-compliance
Lightning Source LLC
Chambersburg PA
CBHW031349040426
42444CB00005B/246